MONOLOGUES ON
BLACK LIFE

MONOLOGUES ON BLACK LIFE

Gus Edwards

HEINEMANN
Portsmouth, NH

Heinemann
A division of Reed Elsevier Inc.
361 Hanover Street
Portsmouth, NH 03801-3912

Offices and agents throughout the world

Performance rights information can be found on p. 158.

Library of Congress Cataloging-in-Publication Data
CIP is on file with the Library of Congress.
ISBN 0-435-07035-5

Editor: Lisa A. Barnett
Production: Melissa L. Inglis
Cover design: Tom Allen/Pear Graphic Design
Manufacturing: Louise Richardson

Printed in the United States of America on acid-free paper
00 99 98 97 DA 1 2 3 4 5 6 7 8 9

Contents

PORTRAITS IN BLACK

MEN

LIFETIMES ON THE STREETS

Introduction

I'VE BEEN WRITING MONOLOGUES for some years now and truly enjoy doing so. I don't view them as "finger exercises," the way some playwrights do. To me they're portraits in miniature that require a lot of thought, time, and careful brush strokes to complete.

From another perspective I guess one could call these monologues photos, snapshot portraits of black life taken from various angles. View this, then, not as a book but as a gallery wherein these life-size miniatures are hung. But unlike photos in a gallery that just sit there inviting inspection, these portraits talk, move, reach, and cry out to us. They solicit our time, attention, compassion, and understanding. But if they demand one thing overall, it is recognition. Recognition of the fact that they are a part of the great drama: life.

All the world's a stage / And all the men and women merely players / They have their exits and their entrances / And one man in his time plays many parts . . . (Shakespeare, *As You Like It*, 11, 1)

And so it is with these characters. They take the stage for a moment, demand the focus of a spotlight and make their plea for recognition, fictional creations though they may be.

The world of black Americans is varied and limitless, or so it seems to me. The spectrum of our experiences is both universal and specific. Universal because we are all involved in the great human parade. Specific because of our history, cultural background, speech patterns, and attitudes.

When I first began writing monologues, my idea was to try and put as many black characters on stage as was possible within a short amount of time and space. The final result was *Lifetimes on the Streets*. The additional challenge was to make the evening feel and act like a play without addressing the traditional elements of a play. There would be no plot, no climax, and no resolution. The characters would not even know each other. The only things were they would have in common was the urban landscape they shared and some element of desperation in their circumstance. I think I cheated a little bit with Mavis because there is a dramatic arc in the progression of her story. (This has been pointed out to me by several actresses who've played the role.) My only excuse is that the character insisted it go that way and I went along.

Lifetimes did well both in New York and other places, and it's constantly being produced year after year. Later on I tried writing a companion piece called *Outside Again,* but decided against it because I didn't want to be restricted by time and space limitations. So I just began writing one monologue after another as the characters came to me without considering what they might have in common or how they would share a stage. Each monologue was written to stand alone as an independent entity. But of course when produced they're always grouped together in one form or another. And this is as it should be. Over the years I've seen them performed in a variety of ways and in a variety of places. Theatres, schools, coffee shops, bookstores, museums and even in nightclubs. The combinations are always surprising. Sometimes they're linked thematically or by gender or however else the presenter deems fit. The lengths, too, have varied from fifteen to ninety minutes and all the stops in between. It then occurred to me that I had stumbled upon a very flexible form, so I continued and will continue writing this way.

In a recent interview I was asked, "When do you write?" And I answered very quickly, "Only when I can't put it off any longer." By that I meant when certain characters and stories occupy my mind and imagination so actively that I can't do anything but release myself from them via the writing process. Once written and then performed, they begin to exist independent of me and I can go on with my life again.

I have a friend in the construction business who likes to say, "Tile is my life." I will parallel that by saying, "Monologues are my life." In my more ambitious moments I like to think that I'm in the process of creating an enormous theatrical mosaic of black American life through monologues. If this is so, then *Monologues on Black Life* is only a first installment with more to come. But, about these matters, only time will tell.

PORTRAITS IN BLACK

WOMEN

Jerks

Kiana, age fifteen

Some boys are such jerks that it don't make sense to even think about them. You let them go their way and you go your own, and that's how it is. The world is a big place with lots of people in it. Everything don't begin and end with one stuck-up individual who thinks that he's too good to even say "Good morning" to a person. I mean you see him in the school yard and you say "Good morning Joey" and the guy look at you like you're some kind a ghost or something. So you say, "How are you on this fine sunny winter's day?" and he start mumbling and twitching like he got some kind of itch.

Now I know he can talk because I see him with the other guys laughing and stuff. And I know he ain't dumb because he's one of the top in his class. So why can't he talk to me like a normal person? Everytime, everytime I look at him or say anything, he just start to get all nervous and funny, like he heard something bad about me that he don't want to say.

Well you can keep your secrets to yourself Mister Mysterious! Cause I don't want to know them.

But it makes me so mad. If a boy likes you, why can't he just have the guts to come up and say so? And if he don't, then tell you that too. But don't just stand around like a shadow on the wall letting a person make a fool of herself by trying to be nice to you.

Listen to this: We were waiting for the bus, Jenny and me. Joey come by and I say "Hey Joey, what's happening?" He say to me, "Nothing much." So I say to him, "Everybody's going to Angie's party, you coming?" He says to me "No." So I ask him why. "I got to work," he say. "I got to work that night." So I say to him, "When don't you work?" He say "Sunday." And that's when I said: "That's funny, I'm not doing anything on Sunday either." Hint, hint . . . know what he said to me? He said, "But that's the day I try to catch up on my schoolwork."

I give up. What more can I do? Throw myself at his feet? Run after him and beg? No, I ain't doing that. Not for him. Not for any man. I got my pride. I may not have much else in this world but I got my pride.

So, later for you Mister Study Bug. Later for you Mister Stuck-up-and-Nervous. We coulda been good for each other. We coulda had a nice thing. But that's your loss, not mine.

I'm going to Angie's party. And I'm going to be with somebody. I'm going to be with Rich. I can't stand him and he's loud. And I'll probably not have a good time. But at least with him I know where I stand.

Some men are such jerks I sometimes wonder why we women even bother trying. Catch you in the next life, Joey. Or the one after that.

Ang'st

Paula, age sixteen

People are always telling me that these are my best years. And I have to tell you, I don't know what they're talking about. I don't have a clue. Because for me it's boring. B-O-R-I-N-G in capitals.

I go to school, I come home, watch TV, fight with my brother and my mom, hang out with friends, sometimes go to a movie or a concert, and that's it. "End of line. Everybody has to get off. This train makes no more stops."

I work down at the video store. People come in there. Mostly kids with their mothers and men with their wives. Guys come in there too. But they're all keeks and geeks looking for Bruce Willis and Arnold Schwarzenegger movies. A lot of them ask for Claude Van Damme too. How are you going to meet anybody interesting in a place like that?

Sometimes my gym teacher comes in. He's a real meal, if you know what I mean. The kind of guy a girl could go for if he didn't have "Miss Tight Buns aerobic instructor" with all her muscles hanging off his shoulder all the time calling him "Honey this" and "Honey that." That's what I mean by boring. Puking too. But boring first.

Kenny came in. I used to think he had some intelligence. I even used to think he was good-looking. Know what he wanted to rent? Cartoons. The kind they show on Saturday mornings. Not even the good stuff. I couldn't believe it so I had to ask: "What do you see that's so interesting in cartoons?" . . . Know what he said? "I don't know. I just like them, that's all." Then he went running out of the store like he had forgotten to turn off the stove at his house or

7

something. (*Mimicking Kenny*) "I don't know. I just like them, that's all." . . . Deep, real deep.

In the movies and on TV you see these really cool guys. But they must all live someplace else, because there's none to be found around here.

So I wind up doing like everybody else. Going to school, coming home, watching TV, fighting with my mom and brother, hanging out with my friends and going to a concert or a movie. It's an endless cycle that keeps going around and going around. And there's nothing I can do about it but wait until it stops. My only problem is: WHEN?!

Bad Date

Steffi, a woman in her mid twenties

Oh God, Oh God, my heart is still pounding. Give me a moment let me catch my breath, okay? . . . Oh God, I still don't believe it. I still don't believe it. The man is crazy. Absolutely crazy. Why didn't I know that before? Why did it take something like this for me to find out?

It's not like he was a stranger. I'd been seeing him for weeks, not on a date, but sorta casual like. He works across the block so we'd meet in the park at lunch hour, feed the pigeons, talk and walk a little bit. So when he asked me out it wasn't any surprise.

We had dinner and I noticed he was drinking a lot. But I figure, "What the hell, it's a Friday night, why not?" After dinner we hit a few places for more drinks. That was kinda fun. And he was spending money like he had just won the lottery. But who am I to complain? A man wants to buy me champagne—I'm not going to stop him. Only problem was every place we went to he got into some kind of argument. If it wasn't with the waiter, it was with another customer. At one bar we went to some guys wanted to beat the hell out of him because he started shouting, "I hate faggots! I hate faggots!" for no reason, but because of me the guy let him go.

I guess I should've gone home by then but for some reason I stuck around. We went up to Grand Central and got on a train. He had this friend in New Rochelle he wanted to visit. He even called the guy to tell him we were coming and I guess the guy musta said "Okay." Again, I don't know why I went. I shoulda gone home, damn me.

Anyway, we sat on the train and everything was quiet for a while. Then he got up and wanted to pull the emergency cord. The conductor came over and told him to sit down and relax. John wouldn't listen and started trying to punch the man. But he was so drunk the old guy knocked him back in the seat, slapped him a couple times and told him to behave himself.

"I'm going to kill that old fool," John kept saying. I told him to forget it and let's just enjoy the ride. But he kept saying: "I'm going to kill him. I'm going to kill him." After a while I stopped listening to him. (*Pause*)

I must've fallen asleep because when I woke up John was gone. When he came back he told me, "I did it. I killed the old fool." And there was this crazy look on his face.

"What'd you do?" I asked. I couldn't believe my ears. (*Pause*) Apparently he hid between the cars and when the conductor was passing through John pushed him off the train.

I said, "Look man, I don't want to know you." He started to laugh, "I don't want to know anybody like you." So I got up and left.

At the next stop I got off and called the police. It turned out to be a big nothing. John didn't kill anybody. I guess he must've tried to mess with the conductor but the man slapped him down again. He was probably hallucinating when he told me that stuff about killing him. But it still scared me.

When I got home there were six messages on my answering machine telling me that I abandoned him and that he was going to get me for it. Then I heard somebody trying to crash through my kitchen window. That's why I came running over here. It's like *Friday the 13th*. I think I made a date with Freddy the Hockey-Mask-Monster and now he's after me.

You can put me up for the night, can't you? After I settle down I'll call the police. But for now, I just want to stop and catch my breath. Is that okay? (*Pauses to catch her breath*) Thanks. You're a real friend.

I Thought I Was Dreaming

Rakel, a woman in her late twenties

I was so alone at the time. And lost. I admit that, I was lost. I just kept bouncing from one situation to another trying to find somebody or some place where I could be comfortable. But I wasn't having any luck. So I was just kinda staying by myself reading and thinking about what I was going to do with my future.

One night I went to this party and met these two guys and this woman who said they were trying to put together this Black Poetry magazine and could use any help I could offer. It sounded kind of interesting. And I thought that maybe I could get some of my own poetry published too. Why not.

So a week later, on a Saturday night, I went to her apartment for our first meeting. There were about six people there. All black. All of them poets too. We talked, made plans, and even read some of our own poetry. There was this one guy with a beard who kept staring at me and staring at me. When he read I thought his stuff was very good and told him so. He didn't have much reaction. He just kinda smiled and said, "Thank you."

They served some wine with cheese and crackers. And we made more plans for the magazine. It was starting to get late and I had to leave. The man with the beard offered to walk me to the subway but I told him no. It wasn't necessary, and I left.

At that time I wasn't living up here. I was living in the Village down on Avenue B. The train took forever and when I got home I was feeling exhausted and dizzy. Maybe

I had drank too much wine. I remember hearing something by the kitchen window but I didn't pay it much
attention. I just took off my clothes, turned off the lights,
and hit the bed.

I woke up suddenly to something touching me. I
thought I was dreaming. But I wasn't. It was the man with
the beard. The poet with the strange eyes. He was sitting
on the bed looking at me. Again I thought I was dreaming.
This didn't make sense. How could he be here? How could
he know where I live? I sat up and tried to shake it off. But
I wasn't dreaming. It was real. Then he started to touch me
again.

"What—what are you doing here?" I asked. "Isn't it
obvious," he said quietly. "I'm going to scream," I told
him. "I'm going to call the police." "No you're not," he
said. "Why? Why won't I call for help?" "Because—you
won't survive it," he said. Then he slapped me so hard I
thought the side of my head would explode. I started seeing double when he pushed me back on the bed and
pressed his weight against me . . . Afterwards, when it was
all over he sat in the dark still staring at me with those
strange eyes.

"Why me?" I asked but he didn't answer, so I asked
him again. "Why? Why did you follow me?" "You were
asking for it," he said. I didn't understand what he meant
but he wouldn't explain. Then he pulled out the phone
and left. I never saw him again. The people for the magazine said they didn't know him either.

That was so many years ago and I guess I should forget
it. But I keep remembering his face and the way it hurt
when he slapped me. And the way it hurt even more when
he put his hand between my legs. Oh God . . . Oh God
. . . I don't think I'll ever forget that as long as I live.

Weird Eyes

Lisata, early twenties

He was sitting like over there. And I was sitting over here
and the train was moving and people was getting on and
off and all the man kept doing was looking at me and
looking at me with these big brown eyes like he was
never going to stop looking at me. I was going to get up
and move to another car then I thought "Why should I,
just because that man want to stare like a fool?" So I continue sitting there looking out the window but I could
feel his eyes on me, making me uncomfortable and
squirmy. So I turn and start to stare back at him. Why
not? He staring at me, I got every right to stare back at
him, make him be the one to feel like somebody looking
right through his clothes. So that's what I did. I looked
straight at him.

Then I couldn't believe it, the man got up, moved
over, and sit down next to me. Right on the same seat.

"Hi," he said. I wouldn't answer. "Hi," he said again.
So then I said to him, "What you want mister? What is it
you after?"

"Civility," he said.

"What's that?" I didn't know what this crazy man was
talking about. "Somebody who's just polite. Who doesn't
treat this place as though it's a jungle," he said. "But it is a
jungle," I told him. "Ain't you heard? New York City is a
jungle, all the tall buildings is trees and all the people in it
animals." "I don't think you're an animal," he said. "That's
because you don't know me." "Are you saying that if I get
to know you, you would devour me?" he asked. "Man, I

don't know what you talking about." . . . "I'd like to get to know you," he said.

"Why?" "Because you're somebody and I'm somebody. And people who are somebodies should get to know each other. That's why." At this point I was so confused I didn't know what to say. First he was staring at me like a weirdo, now he was sitting here talking strange but nice. And for a minute I had this idea of maybe telling him my name. I mean he wasn't bad looking and he had a nice voice when he talked. But then I thought, "Hey, hey—suppose he's one of them serial killer people you read about who ride the subway staring at people, then later following them home and killing them. Or suppose he's a rapist looking for another victim. That's the problem with this city, you can't trust anybody. This friend of mine, Joanne, she met this guy at a dance, took him back to her apartment, let him stay the night and the next morning after he was gone she found out that he had stole all her money while she was sleeping, plus her radio and cassette recorder. I mean, men, most of them, what they really want to do is take advantage of a girl and any situation she give them. Ain't that so? So I told this man that "I think you better go." "Why? I thought we were getting along," he said. "No mister, we ain't getting along. You getting along by yourself, maybe, but you ain't getting along with me. And if you don't leave this seat now I'm going to have to pull the emergency cord and tell the guard when he come over that you bothering me."

He didn't say anything. He just got up and went to another seat. At the next stop he got off and left. I kinda felt sorry for him because he looked down and kinda dejected like. I mean it don't make me feel good to put anybody down or spoil their day. But what could I do? The man had weird eyes.

I got home and told my aunt about it and you know what she say? "Suppose it was Jesus riding that train just trying to talk to people about the state of the world?"

I told her, "Then he was talking to the wrong person because I don't know nothing about the state of the world." Aunt Louise is so crazy. I don't know why I even said anything to her. Jesus, imagine that. Jesus riding the subways staring at people then trying to talk to them. If God is that dumb then he deserve what he get.

Then she said: "Suppose he was that millionaire they used to have on TV who used to go about looking for people to give a million dollars to?" About that time I stopped listening to her.

But that man wasn't no Jesus. And he wasn't no millionaire either. He was just a lonely man looking for company. But you know what the real joke is? I'm lonely too. But I ain't telling Auntie that.

Of Course They Called It a Tragedy

Betsey Mae, a woman in her late twenties

They were searching for a killer, they said. Sure they were. That's exactly who they were eager to find, right. The man who killed the man they were all calling "The Enemy of America," forget that he had whites following him and agreeing with what it was he was preaching. Forget that he had won the Nobel Prize for peace. Forget that he said, "I have a dream that is deeply rooted in the American Dream." Those things were only making them hate him more. Do they seriously want me to believe that the FBI wasn't secretly happy when they heard that he had been shot? That J. Edgar Hoover, that great defender of American democracy, wasn't in some room laughing his head off when he got the news. And that many folks all over the North and South weren't holding secret parties because this thorn in their side had been removed in the most effective way a person can be removed. With a bullet in the face.

Of course they called it a tragedy. And of course they were looking for the man who pulled the trigger. They were searching the cities and scouring the countryside with every resource they had. And with one prayer in their hearts. "Oh God, don't let it be a white man. Let it be one of their own. Some eye-rolling, rabid-looking black loony spouting quotes from Nietzsche and the Koran while waving a pistol in the air. He would of course have to be subdued with about thirty bullets through the heart. Then all would be right with America once more.

They had gotten lucky with Malcolm. It was black men who had done the deed. And perhaps this time, if they prayed hard enough. Maybe—just maybe, lightning might strike twice in the same spot again. And you want me to love you all? Think of you as nice people? Yeah. (*She laughs and exits*)

Mommy Loves You

Cynthia, a woman in her late twenties

I don't know what you do when you have a funny child. The doctor say you got to give him a special kind of love and all the understanding you capable of. I try all that but it don't do any good. He still the same. Dumb, retarded and stupid all the time. Pete say it's alright. But it ain't alright by me.

See—I got a brother start out the same. He was born simple but we didn't find out till he was nearly ten. Kids used to tease me and my sister saying our brother was simpleminded, and we used to fight. He grow up and he still was the same, although he live by himself and can do little jobs. But winter and summer, autumn and spring that man wear the same raincoat and walk around saying (*Articulating carefully*) "Hello. How are you? Fine day we having this day, isn't it?" to everybody he meet. Friend and stranger alike. Sometimes he say it so much you got to shout. "Arnie, shut up! You making me crazy!" Then he stop and look at you saying (*Slowly*) "I'm sorry. Didn't mean to offend. I'll not do it again" in some damn British accent he hear on TV. That's all he ever good for—imitating the cartoons and the other voices he hear on TV. . . . Again, Pete think it funny. But I just look at my brother and I want to cry. . . .

With Junior it's the same thing. He can't talk like Arnie, but he just as simpleminded. You give him food, he throw it all over hisself and the floor. Show him a hundred times and he still make his doo-doo in one of the corners or one of the closets. Then when I take him to the toilet and beat his little behind he just stand there crying, but don't learn a thing. He gon' be just like Arnie. I can see it. People gon' have to shout and call out every time they want him to move . . . . I don't know why I couldn't have a normal child. I don't know what I done to deserve this. Everybody I know have one. More than one. Some even got six or seven. Doreen, my neighbor next door, got more than even she want. All of them normal and sensible. What the hell did me and Pete do wrong. I still don't know.

(*Turning and calling*) Junior, what you up to now! Damn you boy. I swear you gon' kill me one a these days. (*Shouting*) JUNIOR! JUNIOR! . . . Why wasn't you born dead, huh? Answer me that! . . . Why wasn't you a stillborn baby? . . . Oh God, oh God . . . I didn't mean it honey. You know mama didn't mean it. She love you. She just saying them things because she don't want you to grow up strange. Mommy love you. And gon' take care of you. Just try to behave a little bit, please.

And the Winner Is

Althea, late twenties

"And the winner for *Best Actress of the Year* goes to ———."
Applause . . . Applause . . . Applause.

She moves to the center of the stage.

Thank you . . . thank you. This is a moment I've dreamt about all my life and now that it's finally here I can't quite believe it. Maybe when I get home and away from all these lights and all this glitter, I'll pinch myself and it will all become real . . . To say I feel proud is to state the obvious. But to say I also feel humble is to state a fact. There are so many people to thank that I don't know where to begin. But have no fear, I won't take up the time allotted to me, by trying. I'll just say thank you to my mother, my father, my teachers, and those fine people in the area where I grew up. Without their love, inspiration and support I could never have gotten to this place. Thank you all and God bless.

She moves out of center stage.

Well I guess that should do it. My agent will be pleased. His specific instructions were that I should thank the people back home. Especially my folks. It'll show that I haven't forgotten my "roots." "It'll make good press," he said. And as always, he's right. So of course, I'll do it. "Tell them the lie they want to hear." That's always been his advice.

But it would be nice, just once, to tell the truth, wouldn't it?

Moves to the center of the stage again. Spotlight comes on.

Thank you, thank you. This is a moment I've dreamt about all my life and now that it's here all I can say is "It's about time." When considering who to thank for all this the perversity of my memory leads to all the people who treated me badly along the way.

Let's begin with my mother who called me a fool and an idiot for wanting a career in the theatre. "You gon' wind up a slut and a loser," she said and promised that she wouldn't give me one ounce of support until I came to my senses. And she kept that promise. And to my father who backed her up when I spoke to him. "Your mother is right," he said. "You better get all them foolish ideas out of your head." And then went back to reading his newspaper.

And to the neighbors who ridiculed any effort I made at standing up in front of a crowd trying to recite something I had learned. "Take a look at that one. She ain't happy with who she is, trying to be something better."

And to Jerome, the boy I wasn't good enough to be seen out on dates with. But who didn't mind spending money for all them nights in all them motel rooms.

Then when I told him I was pregnant, first he tried to deny it was his, then he had his father talk to me. "Jerome will acknowledge fatherhood of the child and the family will support the child properly. But under no circumstances can you expect him to marry you. Marriage is completely out of the question and you might as well face the fact now."

Fortunately for them I miscarried and the problem ceased to exist. But that was enough for me. I left town with the promise that I'd never be back. No matter what.

But now that I've gotten to this spot and I'm up for

this award I have to go back. Win or lose. They're celebrating a day in my honor. And again my agent says I've got to be present. "You can't turn your back. You can't spurn these people." So I'll do what he says. Why? Because he's the one who provided the inspiration, the support and the savvy, that's gotten me to this place.

So—if you thought I was really acting in that motion picture, wait until you see me in my hometown tomorrow . . . then you'll see what real acting is all about. Now once again, thank you all.

How I Lost Religion

Angela, mid to late twenties

Tell you how I lost religion . . . I'm an actress, see. Been wanting to be an actress for a long time. Now I actually make a living acting. People pay me for it and everything, which is wonderful. But it don't happen overnight. I don't care how it look from the outside people don't just go from being nobodies to being famous just like that. (*Snaps her fingers*) Not that I'm famous or even on my way. I'm happy to be making a living. But the idea of fame in my future isn't a possibility I'm ruling out. The parts and my pay keep getting bigger. And my manager and agents keep talking about what kind of role we should be looking for as my first starring vehicle. But all that is a dream they're trying to manufacture. Me, I'm just trying to keep my feet on the ground and my nose to the grindstone. If I can't say anything about myself, at least I can say I'm a realist.

Tell you why that is.

When I was in my last years of high school I knew I wanted to be an actress. So to find out about it I joined this little theatre troupe in our town. The company was a collection of white, black, Latinos and even some Orientals. People played all kinds of parts. What they now calling "non-traditional casting." I got in and was the newest member of this company. I was sixteen but I knew right from wrong. The play I got cast in was a comedy about a girl who joins a football team and scores the winning touchdown.

Also in the cast was the high school principal, Mrs. Joshua, a beautiful black woman who had more poise than the Queen of England. Every girl I knew wanted to grow up to be Mrs. Joshua. Intelligent, good-looking and well dressed. At thirty-two, she was the youngest woman to hold the job of school principal in our town.

The director in our company, Mr. Berry, was a crazy black man my parents warned me not to get too close to. Not because he might hurt me or anything. But because they said a man crazy enough to try to make a living in theatre is a man who shouldn't be trusted around young people. A mind is a terrible thing to waste.

The other person in our cast was a young minister named Mr. Aubrey who they said was doing such a good job in the community that people were thinking about running him for public office. There were others in the cast, but these were the important ones.

In spite of my parents' warning, I still used to talk about show business with Mr. Berry. And he used to encourage me saying I had talent and that I should develop it.

Reverend Aubrey was so handsome that I couldn't keep my eyes off him. He was light-skinned, muscular, and had green eyes. All the girls I knew was in love with him, and used to ask what it was like spending so many rehearsal hours with him. Well, to tell the truth, it wasn't so exciting. He used to talk about God all the time. And all about his family. He had a wife and three kids. His wife was a plain woman and we could never understand how she managed to catch a good-looking man like that.

One day I went to rehearsal and it wound up just being him and me alone. There was some mix-up in the schedule and nobody else showed. So we worked our scenes and it start to get kinda intimate. I was sure Reverend Aubrey was going to kiss me like I wanted him to, when he stopped and begin to tell me about self-control and resisting sin. I was really, really embarrassed because I had this idea that he had read into my mind. I went home that night and said a whole lot of prayers for the thoughts that had been going through my mind.

Rehearsals went on and I kept my distance from Reverend Aubrey, although he would often look at me as if to say: "I know the kind of pictures running through your mind. And one of these days they're going to get you in trouble."

(*Pause*)

One night late after rehearsal I went to the bus stop, which was maybe a half a mile away. I sat and waited for the bus, which, at that hour of night, didn't have any fixed time. It just came and went as it pleased. I must've been there for twenty minutes when I realized that I'd forgotten my script at the rehearsal studio. We all had keys to the side door so I went back to get it.

When I arrived the place was dark. Everyone was gone. By now it was nearly midnight. I opened the door, turned on the light and I heard a gasp. There on the floor in the corner was Mrs. Joshua and Reverend Aubrey. Both naked and lookin' surprised. The Reverend jumped up and put on his slacks. Mrs. Joshua just covered her face and started to cry.

"What're you doing here?" Reverend Aubrey asked me, angrily.

"My script. I forgot my script."

He picked it up from the counter and handed it to me.

"Listen here, Angie," he said following me out. "You shut up about this, you understand."

"Yes, Reverend."

"You just shut the hell up!"

"I—I promise." With that he let me go back to catch my bus.

To tell the truth, I was so frightened I wouldn't've dared to say a word about it. Plus, even if I did, nobody would've believed me. A minister like Reverend Aubrey and a woman like Mrs. Joshua just didn't do that kind of thing. So I just kept my mouth shut and went on with the rehearsals.

The show opened and we were a big hit. Especially me. Our local newspaper wrote me up. And my parents decided that when I went to school I could major in drama.

Reverend Aubrey did run for public office and is now serving on the city council. Mrs. Joshua and her husband got a divorce but she remarried again. She now is the district Superintendent of Schools. Mr. Berry had a stroke but he's still doing plays, and encouraging people with talent. Me? Well, I told you. I'm a working actress and happy about it. But, what I started to tell you was how I lost religion. You know, I'm not exactly sure. I just know that after that incident, I stopped going to church or saying prayers.

Oh, by the way, this is the first time I ever told anybody about it. So keep it under your hat, okay?

Rats

Dvonne, a woman in her mid thirties

I'm sitting here laughing, because when things fall apart what else is there to do but laugh. Right. I could drink, take dope, or throw myself off a building. But what would be the point. The world would still spin and the rats would still be eating cheese.

Every man I meet is a rat. Some are little rats, some are medium sized rats and some are king-sized rodents. I haven't met any of those in a while but what difference does it make. A rat is a rat is a rat is a rat.

Take the guy that just left me tonight. Nice guy, quick with the jokes, a nice dresser. Got himself a good job at the department store where I work. We went out on three dates and everything felt fine. Tonight I bring him to my place and the whole house of cards falls in. We kiss and try to get intimate and that's when he tells me he's gay. I say that it doesn't make any difference to me, but he says, "Yes it does." So then I ask if he knew this then why did he go out with me? He said he wasn't sure and for some reason he thought that I would be the one to help him clear up his doubts. But I guess I wasn't because he told me he was sorry and quickly escaped into the night. Now this isn't the first time this has happened to me and I'm irritated. No, I'm more than irritated, I'm goddamn mad.

I've been in this city going on four years now and all I ever come across are jerkoffs, misfits, malcontents, weirdoes and mama's boys. Every romance I get into is a rat romance of some kind or another. Aren't there any normal guys in this city anymore? Just straight guys who're looking for a straight woman for just ordinary good times? Like going to the movies, walking in parks or just sitting around drinking coffee and talking. If those people are out there, they must be hiding because I can't seem to find them.

Everyone else I know comes to the city, knocks around for a while, make one or two mistakes. But after the third or fourth, they're locked tight in some terrific relationship that will last at least a year if not a whole damn lifetime. Everybody that is, except me. So I ask myself: What is it about me that puts guys off? Am I a scary person? Do I put too much pressure on them? Should I be more of a wilting flower, instead of the confident, assured person that I am? You know what I sometimes feel like? I sometimes feel like I'm this big black vampire person flying over the city swooping down on men, sticking my fangs into their necks, and sucking out all their blood. At least that's what I think they must think. That's why the good ones avoid me and the losers fall into my trap. They go to the top of the Empire State Building, wave their hands, and I swoop down on them. Sometimes I wish I was that kind of vampire person. Things might be easier. But I'm not and that's my problem.

Sometimes I wish I was gay, but that's a dead-end trap too. I'm not and I would only be lying to myself. My problem is I like men. The long, short, and tall of them. I like their sharp, wet noses, beady eyes, and long slimy tails. My trouble is I keep expecting a rat to act like a person and that'll never be. Like I said before: "A rat is a rat is a rat is a rat. World without end. Amen."

Ahhh—what's the use of crying? Tomorrow is another day. Another turn of the sun. Another new adventure in this maze we call life. I'll go to sleep and wake up with a smile. I'll pretend that today and tonight didn't happen. I'll meet a new rat, he'll put out his paw, I'll shake it, smile and say, "Pleased to meet you." . . . We'll stand there talking for a while and guess what? . . . The whole RAT adventure will start all over again.

How Was I Supposed to Know?

Mabel, a woman in her late thirties

How was I supposed to know?

How was I supposed to know the man was jealous like that? He didn't give anybody a clue. Jeffrey was a man who'd walk around smiling, being easy with everybody. He liked to talk sports. Baseball, basketball, football, boxing. Wasn't the smartest person I ever met, but wasn't the dumbest neither. What I'm saying is, the man was in-between. Now that wife of his, me and her was friends. But Cynthia was always up to something. I don't mean anything bad, but Cinty always had a plan about something. How to make more money, how to get a bigger apartment, how to get a better job. None of the plans ever worked out but she was always scheming. I live just across the street, so she and me used to sit and have coffee before I went to work. She would tell me about these plans and I would tell her, "Yes. Sound like a good idea to me." Then when they didn't work out she would tell me about her new one and I would say "Yes" all over again. That's what friends is for, ain't it? To agree with you.

Me, I don't believe in plans. Plans is a joke. When you have four kids and nobody to support them like I do, you don't make any plans. You take things as they happen— one day at a time.

Last man I been with was more than three years ago. I'm not old and I don't think I deserve to be lonely like this. But when you're a woman with four small children and no husband in sight, every sensible man try to avoid you like a bad accident. Guess they figure that by being with you, that automatically mean they gon' have to start feeding them little mouths. Of course it ain't true. But that's how they figure. Most of them anyway.

I told Cinty about this and she said she had an idea. One of her plans. Said she and Jeffrey would throw a party so I could meet some men. I didn't think it would work, but I said okay anyway. Even put up some money for liquor. What the hell. I'll give anything a shot once.

It was a nice party. Jeffrey got drunk. A lot of men were there. Nobody really interesting except one. A musician named George. Cinty said she used to know him from before she was married. They went to school together or something. He was nice. We talked and danced. Then I invite him over to my place for a nightcap. He came. But all we did was talk, then he said good night. I asked Cinty about him the next day. She said he was like that, quiet and shy. I asked if he was gay or anything. She said she didn't think so then gave me his number to call him.

I'm not shy, I got right on the phone and called. He wasn't home but he had a machine on so I left my number. But he never called. A week went by. Then a second week. Finally I gave up hope. Gave up even thinking or dreaming of what it might've been like to have a man close to me once in a while. You live alone long enough you get used to it.

But imagine my surprise one morning when I went over to have coffee with Cinty to find George there. He was nice and shy like he always was, I guess. But something was funny. What was he doing at her place so early in the morning? Jeffrey had already gone to work, so it was only him and Cinty alone. He said he came to borrow a book. Even show me the book, but I didn't believe them. Cinty was smiling and looking at him too much. I didn't say anything but I thought, "Keep an eye on this."

I live right across the street. I can see right into her window if I put my mind to it. So that's what I did. And I was right. She and George were having a thing. He would go over just after Jeffrey leave, spend a couple of hours, then leave around eleven. Cinty didn't go to work till noon, so she had the whole morning free.

Close as we were I thought she would tell me about it. But she never did. And I got to admit it bugged me. I mean she got a husband sleeping next to her every night and then George coming over there, sometimes four times a week. It didn't seem right, me over here alone and she having one in the morning and one in the night. It just wasn't right. But I kept quiet till one day I couldn't hold it in anymore. So I said something. It wasn't out front, it was slick and diplomatic. . . . I was talking to Jeffrey and I mentioned George. Jeffrey said he hadn't seen him and I said, "That's funny, I thought I saw him coming out of your building the other day around eleven."

Jeffrey said he must've been there to see somebody else. I agreed. But he got a funny look on his face. I didn't even think about it again. I even called Cinty to see about having coffee. But she said she was busy, like she's been busy for the last month or so. Well, when you got that kind of action in your life, who got time for coffee, right? Hmmm . . . (*She laughs*)

Well, next thing I know, one morning I'm looking out my window and ambulance and cops were in front of the place going in and out of the building. A crowd gathered. When I went downstairs a neighbor told me there'd been a killing. Jeffrey had shot George and Cinty, then shot himself. I couldn't believe it. Jeffrey? Nice, smiling Jeffrey? My God.

The papers called it "A crime of passion on the Upper West Side." People talked about it for a while and then it was gone. But I still sit here looking at that window.

It's a funny world we live in. A real funny world. Sometimes you think you know people, but the truth is— you don't know them at all. No sir, you don't even have an idea.

Faithful to the End

Elaine, early thirties

Ain't love great? Ain't love a joy? Want to know something? I ain't ever been in love. No sir, that's a fact. I've heard about it, read about it, dreamed about it, joked about it, but ain't ever felt it. Ain't that a laugh? Thirty-five years old and love is still a stranger to me. . . . I don't know why and I couldn't even begin to guess. I been with a lot of men. Slept with a lot of them, too. It shoulda been love but it always turn out to be something else. Some other game in disguise. Want to know what I think? I think sex is easy and love is hard. But what do I know? I'm just a woman out in the world on her own. . . . Now don't get me wrong. I don't hate men but I don't like them much either. I've never met one that's been nice to me; or even honest. There's always some lie, always some bullshit. And I just don't want to deal with it anymore. I'm tired and I'm drained.

So the only thing left to do is drink. Liquor is the lover who never leaves. And I intend to be faithful to this lover right down to the end. . . . Barkeep, pour me another one, please. . . .

Betrayal

Bess, a boxer, in her early thirties

They paid me and I did it. Didn't nobody put a gun to my
head. And didn't nobody use undue influence either. The
man just came to me simple as that. He comes up and said,
"I have a proposition for you. You can say *yes*, you can say
no. And if you say *no*, there ain't going to be any hard feelings. All I ask is that you hear me out." . . . When a man
talks like that. What do you do? You listen. And that was
my mistake. I listened. (*With sudden passion*) I coulda beat
that woman. Coulda beat her easy. First round I could see
it. She was aggressive and strong, but she was dropping her
left. All I had to do was set a pattern of backing up a certain
way as she came forward, then as my back touched the
ropes, step to the side and nail her. Then nail her again
three or four times before she could get her balance and
then it would be all over. But it was too late for that. I had
made a deal. He was living up to his part of the bargain,
now I had to live up to mine. Still it make me mad. She's
on the cover of *Sports Illustrated*, and me, I'm just a statistic
on her so-called distinguished record. Her next fight is
going to be a main event on SHO. Her purse is three quar-
ters of a mil. The highest paid to a woman boxer so far.
Know what I got for the fight I ditched? Ten thousand legit
and another fifteen under the table. My next fight, if I get
another, will pay four, maybe five if I'm lucky.

In that old Marlon Brando picture where he played a
ex-fighter he said to his brother in that taxi, "You shoulda
looked out for me a little bit. You were my brother. You
shoulda looked out."

I feel a little bit the same way. He came to me, he was a brother with a smile. He was wearing good clothes. And the way he talked you knowed he was college educated. He looked at me, called me Sister, and said we got to look out for ourselves. We got to be educated about the realities of life in America. And one of the realities he said was that no TV sponsor was going to spend any money on an event, that's what he called it, "an event" where a black woman could be seen beating up on a white woman. "What about a white woman beating up on me?" I asked. That's when he said the magic words: "You're a professional. You can keep that from happening. Just waltz for three rounds, let her get in a good one and take a slight snooze. It's worth fifteen grand that you don't have to share with anybody else. No agent, no manager, no trainer, no taxman. Just cash in an envelope and the deal is together." When I said *yes*, he gave me half as a show of good faith. After the fight I got the rest.

He went his way, I went mine. Just another fight as far as I was concerned. But I didn't see the pattern. She was on her way to glory while I was headed for the dumps. Now she's on magazine covers and on talk shows while I'm just trying to pay next month's rent. I look at her on the tube and I can't help but think: "It coulda been me. It shoulda been me. I should be there." . . . But I was a fool. I listened to a Brother with a smile. And now I'm mad because I still think: "You shoulda looked out for me a little bit. You was my brother, you shoulda looked out."

What I Believe

Glenda, in her forties

I didn't know but I had an idea. I mean you don't spend time with a man, have dinner with him, lay up in bed and stuff like that without having some idea of his character. But what I didn't know I guess I didn't want to know. You see, to me there ain't much point in asking questions. The past is the past. What a man done or who he used to be ain't got nothing with who he is now or where he want to go. Time change, people change and that's just how it is. I accept things that way.

James and I met and we were right for each other right from the start. He was a little down on his luck, I could tell that but it didn't bother me. I mean most men I meet are down on their luck in one way or another. Some act mean and nasty about it. Others just walk around all day in a funk, whipped and depressed. But the worst I think are the ones who need to get their heads bad on drugs and booze. I know what I'm talking about because I been with all kinds. And when I tell you James was different you gotta take my word for it. He wasn't optimistic but he wasn't pessimistic either. He was just kinda neutral. Life had its way and he had his. If things weren't working out it wasn't anybody's fault, just a breakdown in communication is what he used to say, "Just a breakdown in communication."

Love, sex, romance, and togetherness was, for me, the best I ever had with anybody. From the first night we were together I knew it was right. I gave him the second set of keys I had to this place and told him he could come and go as he pleased.

James never worked, not in the usual sense anyway. And I never asked what he did. I knew it probably wasn't legal but it wasn't my business or my place to ask. So I just let it be. Many times I would leave him in the house broke when I went off to work. When I came back he'd be sitting there smiling with a new jacket or hat. Or sometimes a present for me. "Let's go out for dinner," he'd say. And that's what we'd do. Wine and dine and talk. He liked to talk about the future. Never the past, just the future. See, he was from the South and didn't like it up here in the city. Told me he'd been in the city too long and needed to get back home. Back to his roots. Told me he wanted me to come back with him, if that's what I had a mind to. I told him, "Sure." Wasn't nothing keeping me here. Nothing I cared much about anyway. So we made plans.

James liked to cook. Said that he used to work short order and was good at it. The plan was to go back home and open a small place. Nothing elaborate. No bar and stuff like that. Just good food with soft drinks to wash it down. Of course, it would cost money, but he didn't seem to be worried. We made our plans. On a certain day of a certain month without saying "boo" to anybody we would just pick up and go. I didn't ask why, I just said I would be ready.

And I was ready too. Ready and waiting and waiting and waiting and waiting. Evening turn into night, then night into morning, then back to evening then night again. "James wouldn't do this," I told myself. "He wouldn't lie and just abandon me like this. There got to be a reason. Got to be an explanation. I know I ain't that bad a judge of human character." So I waited some more. Didn't go to work, didn't leave the house. Just sat there and waited.

If I had turned on the TV, I guess I would've known. People said it was on TV just after it happened. But I hadn't so I didn't. I saw it in the paper two days later. Story about James and his friend Gregory and the so-called shoot-out they had with the cops. I say "so-called" because eyewitnesses say they didn't see Gregory or James with any weapons firing back at the cops. All they saw was them trying to run and the two cops shooting at them.

Four bullets in James and three in Gregory. I didn't know Gregory but that doesn't matter. He was a friend of James, and that's enough for me. Cops say they were responsible for all kinds of crimes including drug pushing and murder. And every day since the incident they adding more to their list. I guess they didn't know about me since nobody's come to knock on my door.

He's gone and I'm sorry. I loved him, and I don't believe all that stuff. The police are goddamn liars. He wasn't no hit man and no hotshot pusher. If that was so, why was the man broke all the time? . . . Tell you what I believe and I ain't got nothing to prove it either. It's just what I believe. I think James tried something. He musta got in with some slick operator and made a try at a big payday. This is the money we woulda gone away on. But it wasn't to be because it was a setup. A setup between Mr. Operator and the cops. And that's why they had to kill them, so they wouldn't talk.

Like I say, that's my own theory and I got nothing to back it up. But that's what I believe.

Some world we live in, ain't it? . . . Yeah, some world.

Top of the World

Nishell, a woman in her forties

Ever since I was a child I wanted to be a movie star. I'd see those people up on that big screen and think to myself: "Hey that's what I want, to be up on that big screen, smiling and talking, looking all wonderful." And like a fool I started saying it to everybody. "When I grow up I'm going to be a movie star. . . . When I grow up I'm going to be on TV too."

As long as I was a child the family and folks around the neighborhood let me go along talking up that stuff. But when I start to get to the age where they figure I should have some common sense people started telling me I should shut up about that nonsense. "Don't you know there ain't no such thing as a black movie star?" "What about Dorothy Dandridge and Abby Lincoln? What about Sidney Poitier and Sammy Davis, Jr.? What about Ruby Dee and Ossie Davis?" I would ask hoping to stop the argument they was giving me. "Them people was lucky and some of them got talent. People like Sammy Davis was born into show business and knew the right people. You ain't got none a them connections." "What about Diana Ross?" I asked. "Girl you got to be joking. Don't you see how beautiful Diana Ross is? Don't you hear how good she sing? You just a poor black girl who better learn her lessons and get your head outta them clouds." So I tried but the dream never left me. Nothing ever attract me like the idea of acting and being in the movies. But mama said I'd better be practical if I want to make my way in this world. "Movie business is a fantasy, you involved in reality. You hear me child? Stop being a dreamer." So I decided I would become a nurse. And mama broke her back working to pay my way through nursing school. When I graduated it made her proud to say, "My daughter is an RN. Registered nurse is next to being a doctor." And she remained proud of that till the day she died.

But I've never been proud of it. I've never even cared. Nursing to me is a way to make a living and a complete waste of time. I go to the movies just about every day. And from every corner of the screen I see people like me doing what I had dreamed about doing until all those fine, loving, well-meaning people talked me out of it. Teased me out of it with nicknames like "The African Marilyn Monroe" and "Miss Elizabeth Taylor of Sheba." I want to be up there with them doing what they're doing but it's now too late. I'm forty-two and married with children and a husband who left me. I lived out my mother's dream but forgot about my own. Something went wrong somewhere and I was a fool. Now it's too late. . . .

So I've decided I may not be able to really be in the movies but I can dream about it like I used to do when I was a child. Now of course I need a little help to dream so I use this. (*Shows a bottle*) A few sips when the theatre gets dark and me and the people on the screen are one and the same. I look like they look and do what they do. When I leave the theatre everything's fine. I can go home and deal with the world and its nonsense.

Deal with the reality everybody told me I was avoiding when I was dreaming about a life in the movies. (*Holding up her bottle*)

"Top of the world, mama . . . Top of the world! . . ." I finally made it to where I wanted to be, "top of the world." I hope you're proud.

Secrets

Children make me laugh sometimes. They like to think they inventing the world. That the first time they discover something that's the first time it begin to exist. My boy Roddy ask me to sit down today. Said he had something he had to talk to me about seriously. I kind of had an idea it was coming. He's been trying to set me up for this talk all week. I could see him looking at me closely, waiting for when the time was right I suppose. I didn't say anything. I just let him work it out. And I guess this afternoon was the time. He sat me down in the kitchen when nobody was around and asked me to listen. Listen very carefully.

So I said: "Alright, Son, I'm listening. I'm listening very carefully." Then he held his breath, hesitated for a very long time and then said, "Mama, I'm gay. I've been gay for a long while now and I don't want to keep it a secret any more. I want to go public with it."

"What do you mean, 'You want to go public'?" I asked.

"I've found a man I love and I'm going to move in with him."

"And this man," I asked, "how does he feel about you?"

"He says he loves me."

"I see."

"Sooo—what do you think?" he asked with more concern than I've ever seen on his face before.

"Well," I said, "I think it's wonderful."

"You mean you ain't upset?"

're my son
me—your

id, hugging
understand-

are for. Not
upport them
see it was a

don't they? I
child. But at
. What did he
him? Bang my
s mother better
't know that he
heaven's sake. I
her not to know
and dislikes and
led to talk to me
't do it sooner. I
cked. That since I
that to me would
g.
ugh. They act like
you didn't have _____ orn. That your life
and theirs began simultaneously. That everything they
telling you is new information . . . sure. Why not. A par-
ent doesn't have to tell her child everything. She's allowed
to keep a secret here and there. That's what gives us depth
and dimension, I suppose. The little secrets we keep.

Mine was called Janet and I was twenty-three when we
started our relationship. She was twenty-six. We lived
together for three years. People thought we were room-
mates and that was fine with us. I thought about telling
my parents and would've if things didn't start to come

apart with Janet and me. Small things at first and then they got bigger. Finally there was nothing left to do but separate. She went to Europe and then moved to Seattle. I stayed here. It took a while to get over it, but I did. That's when I met Warren, Roddy's father. We got married, had Roddy and the two girls and had settled down quite nicely when the accident happened. Wasn't anybody's fault. The tunnel flooded, Warren was in there working with six other men. They all drowned. His insurance paid us a lot of money, so on that level, things haven't been bad. But money is no substitute for a person, I don't care how much of it there is.

(*Pause*)

Janet is a psychiatrist. She still lives in Seattle. She never married. Every year at Christmas she sends us a card and a present. And on everyone of the kids' birthdays she sends them a check. They know her as "Aunt Janet," Mommy's friend whom they've never seen. . . . I know her as more. Much more.

MEN

Social Intercourse

Jaims, age sixteen

Want to know how to make a million dollars? I'll tell you
how to make a million dollars. No, you don't have to kill
anybody or get a hit record. Or any of that usual other
stuff. . . . All you have to do is write a book or make a
video on what to say to a girl you like after you said
"Hello." And that's what it could be called: *What to Say to
a Girl You Like After You've Said Hello. . . .* Because it ain't
easy. And I know that there's a lot of guys out there like me
who would like to read such a book. At least one million
would be my guess. And if each one of us bought the book
or the video, well—you see what I'm talking about.

You know, it's funny. In school they try to teach you a
whole lot of things. But they don't teach you that. *Intro to
Social Intercourse,* they would call it, I'll bet you everybody
would enroll.

Now get the picture. I'm standing in the school yard
and she was looking at me. I think she was. I'm hoping she
was but I can't be sure. I mean I could feel something,
somebody staring at me. I look at her but I can't be sure.
. . . What if she was just looking at that sign in back? Or
that billboard across the street? Suppose she wasn't looking
at me at all, but at the fence and at all the cars passing by
on the street? I'd feel like a fool going up and saying something to her. Girls can be so stuck up sometimes.

And if I did say something, what would it be? Hello?
. . . So I say "Hello," then after that—what? That's what I
mean. That's where the book would come in handy.

Oh Lord, oh Lord, I better take this slow. Back up a

little bit . . . I like her. I even know her name. It's Gwen. I know her friends but I don't know her. Now she's over there and I'm over here and I want to talk to her. More than that I'd like to go out with her. Take her to the movies and stuff. Kiss her, touch her, tell her jokes, and watch her laugh. I . . . I . . . I would even like to—oh Lord, I don't even want to think about it. It wouldn't be possible anyway. I come up with something like that and she would probably just laugh in my face.

Still, I'd like to know her. Talk to her just once even. Just once.

Bertie and Scratch say I should just walk up to her, put my arm around her, squeeze her and say, "Yeah mama, you hot." Oh yeah, that would get me in real good. Real tight. . . . Friends, you talk to them about a serious problem and that's the answer you get. Dumb jokes and bad advice. Thanks guys, thanks a lot.

But that don't change things. I'm still here and she's still over there. So what do I do?

Somebody hurry up, write that book please. I can't stand here forever. And I need help . . . Help . . .

Report from Here

Val, a man of nineteen

Hey Joe,
You wouldn't believe this city if you lived here. I can't believe it and I do. Every corner you turn at rush hour, there's this army of young sexy foxes coming at you in all sizes, all colors, and all ages. Sometimes if you quick, you can talk to one of them. Talk to more than one sometimes. Get their phone numbers even. But that can get old soon. These big city chicks only after one thing from a man. Security and a nice wedding ring. Same as the chicks back home. But like we used to say: "When you made of Teflon, don't nothing ever stick to you." So I'm cool and clean. Still lean and mean. But get this for weirdness if you want to hear something real off the wall.

About a month after I got here I was down in the Village sitting in the park just watching all the people and hanging out when this chick come over and start talking to me. A good-looking damsel with long dark hair and big brown eyes. First question she ask was if I believe in free love and things like that.

I told her that I didn't know. Since the kinda town I come from nothing was for free. Everything you had to pay for, even the stuff that was supposed to be for free.

She told me that was a shame and said that she belonged to a church that only worshipped and celebrated things of the flesh. "Other churches deal with the spirit, we deal with the flesh." And then she ask if I wanted to go to a church like that. I said "Hell yes" and wrote down the address as fast as she could talk.

That night I went to the number she gave me. It was in a warehouse on a dark street up on the twentieth floor. Inside, the room was like a little church with benches and an altar. The Reverend, Minister, or whatever he called himself was standing there naked, reading from this Indian book: *The Kama Sutra,* while the people on the benches was touching and kissing and making it with each other. It was kind of a nutty scene. There was women and women, men and men, as well as men and women, making out. The chick who invited me came over and said: "Hey, I see you made it." I smiled, she took my hand and after a while we started to kiss. Before I knowed what was happening we was lying in a corner going at it like everybody else while that naked Minister just continue reading and talking.

After a while the girl get up, fixed her clothes, and said, "I got to go," and left. I was tired so I left too.

When I got home I went to sleep. When I woke up it was like it really didn't happen. I kinda dreamed the whole thing up. So the next night I went down there again. I found the building but I couldn't get in. Everything was locked up and dark. I pushed the buzzer like I had the night before but wasn't any answer. Man, I tried for a whole week but that church was gone forever and ever. Everyone I ask say they never heard of it. When I tell cats here, they say it's a lie. Say I been seeing too many movies, reading too many strange books. But I swear to God it was true.

This city man, if it ain't a little piece of Heaven then it got to be some kinda corner of hell. I don't know which. Anyway, that's the latest report from this soldier in the field.

Write when you get the chance, tell me what's been happening with you.

Your Buddy,

Val

A Pledge and a Promise

Luke, a man in his late twenties

I just got out man, but to tell you the truth, I don't care anymore. At the gate, warden shook my hand, said I paid my debt to society, then wished me luck. "Luke you got it in you to be good. Don't mess up like you did before and yours could be a happy and productive life." While he was saying that I could hear the two guards behind him snickering. "He gon' be back," they were saying. "That fool can't play it straight and honest. He gon' be back in less than a month. I'm willing to bet money on it."

Well, they're wrong. I won't be back—ever. And Warden Wilson is wrong too, because that straight and narrow business don't pay. Not if you're black. That "straight and narrow" business just make the white man feel safe with you is all. Just make him think you're a "good nigger." And he don't have to worry about the safety of his wife and kids when you around.

But I got news for you, man. You better be scared when I'm around because I'm declaring war on you for all you done to me and mine since the day I was born right up to now. I could go back further than that to the way you treated my father and grandfather. The way you raped, abused, and disrespected my sister, mother, and grandmother. But I'm keeping it strictly personal and only holding you accountable for what you done to me.

From day one you made me have to go to the worst school with the worst teachers. Teachers who cared for only one thing, their paychecks. So that even when I tried there was no place to go but sideways. Never up, only sideways. Not even down 'cause I was already at the bottom.

When I got out of high school the best job I could aspire to was a clerk in a supermarket. When I asked about college I was told, "Your marks ain't up to no college standard." So I took the job in that supermarket. One day the manager accused me of stealing to cover the fact that he was the one doing the deed. When I hit the lying bastard in the mouth I was put in jail for assault.

When I got out I had no job. For a while I tried to believe that I could actually make it without getting into crime. But an empty belly and a head full of liquor don't listen to too much reason. That's when me and the boys tried to rob that little bank in Cable City. Bank robbery, even if you don't get spit, is a federal offense. Nine years in that hellhole locked up with all kinds of killers and perverts, including a lot posing as guards. Got out with six for good behavior. But believe me, it wasn't easy.

Now I'm out I intend to raise some hell. But it ain't how you think. I ain't doing it with a gun. A man who pick up a gun is a damn fool. What is it the Bible say? "Them live by the sword shall perish by it." Well it's the same with a gun. Plus, that's what the man hoping for. Me to pick up a gun so he can have an excuse to shoot me down.

No Mister White, that's not what I'm aiming to do. I'm picking up a more dangerous weapon than a gun. I'm picking up a book. See—inside I started to read and take courses. I know now what I want and I know how to go after it. I'm going to study law and I'm going to fight you in the courtroom. I'm going to fight you in the classroom too. But mostly in the courtroom. I'm going to teach you the meaning of justice like you never learned it before. So look out Whitey I'm preparing on becoming your worst nightmare. "A nigger with an education!" You don't believe me? Just wait and see.

The Outsider

Odam, a man in his mid twenties

I hate this city, I really do. It ain't bad enough that it deprives you of everything but the bare necessities of life. But it also got to show you what it is you're being deprived of. So if you can't afford a car (which of course don't make sense in this city since there ain't no place to park) it's wall-to-wall cars wherever you look. Mercedes, Ferraris, Porches, BMWs, fantail Caddies and every kind of sports-car you can imagine. All of them shiny, buffed-up, and new. All of them with some pretty girl with long hair who you would kill your parents for, sitting in the front seat next to the driver. One more way for this city to tell you "Some got it, but you don't, loser."

Or if you live in a hovel, as I do. Then it's all these glassed-in doorways where women with their dogs walk in and out while doormen in gloves and uniforms touch their hats and open the doors for them, as if them women couldn't open the doors for themselves.

It's hell being out here on the street but I ain't got no place else to go.

The place where I live everybody there is like me. Broke, depressed, down all the time. Everybody got a job. None of us is criminal or anything like that. But after the rent is paid and money is took out for food there ain't that much left for any kind of luxury. So those of us who don't hang out in bars stay home and watch TV night after night till it's time to go to sleep. If you watch TV on any kind of regular basis you know how much fun that got to be. Boring, boring, boring.

Weekend like this sitting around the house is more than dull. It's deadly. So I walk down the street looking at all the things I hate this city for.

I look at the fine clothes in store windows. I look at the fine women walking up and down the streets. I look in on all the nice restaurants I can't afford to go into. Look at all the fine stereos and TVs and VCRs in the showcases. And dream of a time when all of that'll change.

This is the agony and the ecstasy of living in this city. I love it and I hate it. But most of all I just want to belong. I just want it to love me like I love it. Now I want to know is that too much to ask?

Dog Nights

Ben, mid to late twenties

Anyway, anyway, so I get to this audition, see? And guess who's there? Right, right. The same woman. I ain't joking. I mean four different places my agent send me and four times I run into this same sweet-looking beast. And I mean she is down, baby, down. Whoa. My engine start to sputter and purr. And my mind start to think about all kinds of possibilities. All kinds of possibilities. Forget about the audition, forget about the part I'm up for. Forget about the money I could make if I get even one of these parts. All I want to know is who this woman is, what's her name, and how we could get to know each other good. I mean real good. Damn, opportunity was staring me in the face and I had to do something about it fast. Real fast. That clock don't strike but once and you got to make your move, or else forget it. You follow what I'm saying?

My mind start to race. "Talk, talk" it kept saying to me. "Talk before they call her in. Say something. Make contact idiot." . . . Only problem was, I didn't know what to say. I mean she's sitting there, I'm sitting here less than four feet away and not one intelligent sentence is going through my mind to say to this lady. That's when I wish I had read more books, gone to more movies or something. Anything that would help me think of something to say. Heck, I'm supposed to be an actor, right? I'm supposed to know how to talk. So that's what I'm going to do, talk. So I go over to her and I say, "Hey, this is the third or fourth time I've seen you in two days. Are you following me, or is it me who's following you?" . . . Dumb, right? Dumber than dumb. But guess what? She look at me with those big eyes, those full lips and all that hair and she smiled. This Amazon goddess smiled and said, "Yes, it kinda looks that way, don't it?"

Wow! Wow! The door is open now at least. So we talk about auditions, talk about acting, and all kinds of other things. But most of all we talk about dogs. Turns out this woman is crazy about dogs. I mean dogs are okay with me, but no more than that. But to keep the conversation going I tell her I love dogs. Think they're the best animals in the world. Stuff like that.

They call her in to audition. She goes. Now it's my turn. I ask her if she'll wait till I come out.

Why? She ask. "Because I want to hold you and kiss you and squeeze you and take your clothes off, then take my clothes off. You know all that stuff." Nooo, I didn't say that. That's what I wanted to say. But I played it soft. I just said, "I don't know—I'd just like to talk some more about dogs with you and stuff."

She said okay.

Turns out she's not even an actress. What she is, is a model. A showroom model. But somebody told her she should try her hand at acting. So she started making the rounds.

We talk, drink coffee, talk some more. Coffee talk turn into dinner conversation. After dinner we go to this little piano bar, listen to some music and drink some more. I'm listening to her talk about this dog of hers named Storm and somewhere in the middle of things I say, "I would sure like to meet that dog of yours." "You mean that?" I tell her, "Yes. I wouldn't of said it if I didn't." So then and there it was settled. I would be going back to her place. Can you believe that? A few hours ago we were strangers at an audition. Now she was inviting me to her pad. And there are those who like to say dreams don't come true.

We got to her apartment and this big dog comes up to me. I was kinda scared for a moment, but the dog is so friendly you can't help but like him. We got along fine. And she is so pleased she pours me a drink. And the next thing I know, we're all over each other. Clothes one way, underwear another and it's *Thunder Over the Plains* starring Randolf Scott and Lex Banker on the late show. When that was over there was more thunder and that sequel followed by another and another. Finally I had to say, "Whoa, I need me a little bit of sleep just to build my strength back up, then I'll be ready to go again." So we went to sleep, woke up early, and started up again. . . . After that we showered together, dried each other off and she said she would make breakfast. That's when I started looking for my clothes. They were all over the place. Then my eyes hit the corner next to the sofa. My wallet was there chomped in three pieces lying on the floor. And the money I had in it, close to three hundred dollars all chewed up and wet in little tiny balls. My money. My pay. All the money I had in the world in little tiny pieces. And the dog in the corner still chewing on more of it.

I didn't know what to do. I wanted to yell, scream, jump out of the window. But I didn't do any of those things. I just called out to her and—point to the dog.

Of course she said she was sorry . . . And of course I said it was alright. What else you going to say? She even offered to pay for it but I said no. Wasn't her fault. Plus, to tell the truth, I don't think she had the money.

That dog. That damn, damn dog. I wanted to—Ahhh, what's the point?

My problem is I need a favor. I can't tell Claire this story. I'm going to have enough problems explaining why I been out all night. So if you could just advance me a couple hundred dollars. I don't need all three, just two, I'll get it back to you the early part of next week. I promise.

Biff! Biff! Biff!

Kalid, a man in his late twenties

Yeah—so he says to me, "I'm paying all this money and I got to say please, too?" And I told him, "That's right, Mister, you not only got to say please, but you got to act civilized, too. Else I ain't serving your ugly face and that's a fact."

See, just 'cause you working as a waiter some people got it confused and think of you as their servant.

Well, this cat didn't want to hear nothing of it. He just comes off that chair like a rocket. Teeth all snarling. Nose running snot and everything. Made a big grab for me but I stepped to the side and nailed him with the jab (*He demonstrates*) Biff! Then I nailed him again. Biff! Biff! Biff! Three in a row. Same jab, same place. Cat look baffled but he still was coming at me. So I step to the left and dig with the hook right up under his armpit. He looked at me like he was lost, so I fired about ten in his face. Mop! Mop! Mop! Cut over his eyebrow open and his nose start to bleed. But don't you know, that fool was still coming at me?

(*Pause*)

What? Hell no. Didn't nobody try to stop it. Ain't nothing them people in that place like better n' watching two cats go at it. And this fool Albert big as he was had a rep he had to protect. Now before me he ain't ever had to fight. He just scare folks just by looking at them. But you see, I'm from Missouri. *You got to show me.*

Now after I messed up his face the clown start to grunt and swell even bigger then he was. I thought to myself, "Oh, goddamn I'm in a mix with one a King Kong's relatives." But I couldn't back down. Women were watching. You know what I'm saying? So I did what my trainer always used to tell me. Go for the softest part of the man. In this fool's case it was his gut. So I sink one right in the pit. Boof!...Goddamn, it felt good. Like punching into a pillow. Before he could hold me I sink four more in. I could hear the women at the bar squealing with excitement. And I thought to myself, "Do something pretty, make them love you even more." So I switch hands. That always looks nice. Hit two with the left, switch up to the right. Double up on the jab and get a rhythm going. (*Demonstrates*) Ping!—Pang!—Ping!—Pang! Poop! Poop! Poop! Throw the right foot behind the left, duck at the waist and come up in a graceful circle. . . Truth is, if you put some music to it, you could even call it a dance. See what I'm saying?. . . Huh? . . . No. That didn't stop him. Cat was still coming.

Now I got to confess something my trainer always used to tell me. He always used to say, "Don, you ain't got no punch. You don't hit hard, but you hit damn regular." See, I got fast hands. So that's what I was doing. Hitting him with my fast hands.

But I got to tell you. I was getting tired, and he wasn't getting discouraged. If anything, he was getting madder. And wanted to get a hold of me more. I thought, "Damn, I got to end this thing now." So I took a chair to break it over his head. But the cat was quicker than I thought and he had me in a grip like a bear hug. Then he start to breathe and squeeze. I could feel my ribs begin to crack. I began to panic, and think, "Oh, Jesus Christ, I'm going to die here. This man is going to kill me for sure." My feet was off the ground and this crazy man was bellowing like an animal and crushing my kidneys while forcing my spine to meet with my stomach. I didn't know what to do, so I bit him. I sink my teeth into his shoulder blade and kept biting till I could taste his blood. For a minute, I didn't even think he was feeling that. Then he let out this scream and start hopping up and down in pain. Of course, he let me go and start holding his shoulder. Well, I didn't wait for change. I just took that chair and whooped him with it. When he didn't fall I said, "That's it. I ain't hanging around no more. This thing ain't a man. This is a robot or something I'm tangling with." So I took off. Didn't look 'bout my tips. Didn't say nothing to nobody. Just high-tailed it out that door and down the avenue.

What?

Hell, yes. Gave up the room where I was staying and just lit out for the street. Didn't have that much anyway. Just a radio and some shirts. Noo, I didn't go back to the job either. Hell with the pay. They can keep the pay . . . See, when you beat a cat like that, especially the way I work him over in front of women and all—you got to know that cat is going to get you. If it ain't today, it damn sure gon' be tomorrow. This man knew my name and where I live. And even if he didn't, you can be damn sure somebody gon' tell him.

Now, I may be dumb, but I ain't no fool. I want to live to old age and die in bed like everybody else. So I got in the wind. And I'm still in the wind. It 'bout four months now. I can't say it's fun living hand to mouth. Looking back down every street I walk. But I'm still in one piece. And that's all that counts.

Hey, it was good seeing you. I'll catch you again one day soon.

(*Pause*)

Yeah, I been talking to my trainer about a comeback. Thing is, I got to be careful. I mean, suppose I step into the ring one of these nights under all them lights and this cat jump out of the audience with a gun or something.

See what I'm saying?

A cat can't be too careful, if you know what I mean.

The Speedboat

Zeke, a man in his late twenties

Hey, I don't apologize for what I do or who I am. I ain't ashamed. I am who I am and proud of it. You don't like it, too bad.

So I live by my wits. Big deal. There's a whole lot of people out there who wish they could live the way I live and survive. But they can't. Me, I ain't only making it, but I'm living damn good. Wake up when I like, go to sleep when I want. And ain't no bossman there to tell me different.

Yeah, I used to do that 9-to-5 jazz, but I gave it up. That was losers route. A dead-end street for cats going nowhere except in a big circle. I ain't one of them and never been.

Last regular job I had was parking cars in this midtown garage. Worked in that place for over a year making bird feed for pay and dog food for tips. That's because I was listening to some woman telling me, "You got to do something decent if you want people to respect you." I musta been in love. That's the only reason I can figure that I stayed in that nothing job breathing in all them poison fumes for so long, trying to please that woman.

Now, don't you know, one day when money was missing I was the one they up and blame. I wasn't near their damn money. Didn't know it was even there. Maybe if I did I might thought about getting my fingers on some of it. I ain't no fool and money is money, right? But the fact is, I didn't take it. There I was walking around innocent but they still decide to put the blame on me. No proof, no evidence but I was the one they point a finger at and let go.

"Why me?" I asked the boss. "I didn't do anything." "There were discrepancies," he said. "What kind of discrepancies?" "Just discrepancies. I'm sorry but I have to let you go."

I was going to push it and make that man explain why he was calling me a thief without any proof. Maybe even call a lawyer and sue him. Then I thought to myself: "You must be some kind of fool to be standing here arguing with this man about this nowhere job in this airless garage." So instead of arguing I just start to smile, shook the man's hand, and told him, "Thank you." He was one baffled-looking cat when I walked outta that place.

When I got home and told my old lady she said I shoulda argued. "It wasn't about the job it was about your pride," she told me.

"Fool's pride," I tried to explain but she came back with, "Man's pride. A man's got to have pride and not let people push him around."

"You right," I told her. And that night I packed my things and got out of that place. Since then I been on my own and ain't never regret it.

The hustle's been good to me. So what do I need a job for? Or love? Hey, I'm like one a them little speedboats you see in the harbor cutting through all them big ships. I make my score and I'm out of there. Here last night, gone this morning. Only thing left is a little ripple in the water where I used to be.

Snakes

Willie, a man in his late thirties

I don't like snakes. Never had and never will, it's as simple as that. I don't see any reason why they on the planet. I know there must be a reason, but I can't see it.

People I know tell me it's ridiculous to be afraid a snakes. But I can't help myself, I been that way ever since I was a kid. People show me a snake, dead or alive—I don't care, and I'm gone from that spot.

When I was in the Army guys used to put dead snakes in my bed just to see me jump a mile. One day I caught a fellow doing it, when I try to put a bullet through his back then people knowed I was serious about not liking snakes.

This last woman I was going out with, Brenda, she had a snake for a pet. A python named Archie. You ever hear stuff like that? Naming a snake as though it was human. Said it was her lucky charm. Used to carry it around in her purse talking to it and showing it to people. Thing wasn't but so big but I didn't like it. So I told her up front: "Look, me and snakes don't get along. Truth is, I am afraid a them, and I can't stand for them to be near me. But, you like the snake, he's your pet and everything like that, so I ain't going to say nothing. Just keep that thing outta my way and the world will be fine."

And she did. At least for a while. A long while. Then one night late after we came from dinner and having a few drinks we was lying out in bed with the lights off talking and listening to music on the radio. That kind of quiet time in the city when you can't even hear traffic anymore. I was kinda falling asleep when I feel this lump move. I turn and it was this goddamn snake trying to work it way under my arm. Goddamn! Goddamn! It musta got outta its cage or something. Jesus Christ, I didn't know what to do. I jump outta that bed and run to the bathroom because to tell the truth, I was about to pee myself from fright.

When I come out Brenda was sitting up with the lights on petting that thing and talking to it. "Oh Archie, why you scare Willie like that? How'd you get outta your cage anyway, you bad boy."

I couldn't believe that. But I didn't want to say anything either. So I just got my clothes from the other room, put them on and left. I don't know if she even realize I was gone. That's how busy she was talking to that snake.

I never went back and she never call. So that was it. A nice situation broken up all because of a goddamn snake.

See, I don't believe it was an accident that it was a snake who messed up the scene in the Garden of Eden. I mean the place was paradise. Adam and Eve had everything good till that snake come in to spoil it. Now for you and I to see paradise we got to die first. Why? All because of a goddamned snake. No. I don't want to see another one. Ever.

Paranoia

Casey, a black man in his thirties, comes running in all out of breath.

I'm sorry to barge in on you like this, but you got to help me. . . . One minute, let me catch my breath. (*Takes several deep breaths*) Ahhh . . . Ahhh . . . alright. That's better.

Damn! Damn! Just when everything was going so well. Just when I was beginning to see my way clear. Just when I was beginning to settle down those bastards show up. It's like they've got it all figured out. Chase you for a while, then fade in the background. Then—just when you begin to forget that they even exist, they show up and start chasing you again.

Who? You asking who? I don't know who they are. But I've seen them before. I've gotten away from them before. Escaped is more the word really. I've escaped from them so many times before I thought they'd given up. Thought I'd lost them. It's been a while. Years even. Then all of a sudden Pop!—out of nowhere, they show up again.

I was walking down the street minding my own business—I don't even remember where I was going anymore—I look across the street and there they are. Those two bastards in their business suits. I saw them just at the exact moment when they saw me. I even saw the one bastard point at me. So I took off. Ran down the street, cut down an alley, and ducked into a couple buildings. Tried to see if they were close behind, but those bastards are slick. They're out there hiding, I know it. They just won't let me see them.

So I hid until it got dark then I dashed across the street against the light, ran down by the river, and came over here. I think I lost them but it's only temporary. They're going to be back, I know it.

You were the closest, that's why I came here. You got to help me out. You got to let me lay low for a while until I can recoup my resources. I can't go back to my place. You're all that's left. Don't turn me out please. Please. It'll just be for a couple of days, then I'll be out of your way. I promise.

Looking around suspiciously he goes toward the back and finds a corner to sit in as the lights fade.

Four Wives

Harold, a man of thirty

Hey look, I'm sorry. To each of you I'm sorry. I know you all hate me and you got good reason to. And I don't blame you, and I apologize. I'm sorry. But in another way I ain't sorry at all. If I didn't love you and was just using you I would be sorry. Sorry in one kind of way. And I said "I'm sorry." But I'm sorry because I love you, each and every one, and I don't like to know that anyone I love is unhappy, for any kind of reason. Especially when it turn out that I am the cause of all this unhappiness. Man, if I could just turn the clock back, move back the pages of the calendar or any damn thing to turn time back, I would do it so I could undo all the harm everybody say I done. But I can't, so I just have to face the music and take my punishment like a man. . . . I said I was sorry but I wasn't sorry. Let me explain what I mean 'bout not being sorry. I'm not sorry because I got to know each of you and got to be loved back in return. When they take everything from me, that's something they'll never be able to take. Those memories, those feelings, those days, those nights, and all the wonderful hours of pleasure we were able to give to one another over and over again. Ladies, I know you hate me but think of those times too. If they were gold to me they had to mean something to you too. Don't let all these newspaper stories, and those cops, and those friends and those ministers and all those other people putting me down spoil it for you. What we had was good, when it was good and we should treasure it always.

Now I got me a lawyer here who tell me I should plead

insanity in order to get a lighter sentence. He figure that
any man who would marry four women at the same time
got to be insane. Or if he ain't insane at least he could con-
vince a jury that he is. . . . Well, I ain't pleading nothing
like that. Because for one, I wasn't insane. I damn well
knew what I was doing. And for another, if I did that I
think it would be a real betrayal. A betrayal of the love I
had and still have for each of you. I wasn't insane. I was
very sane. Too sane maybe. And that's why I did it. Out of
too much sanity.

Janet, when I met you I thought this was it. I had
reached the end of my rainbow and found my pot of gold.
And I did. You was everything I dreamed you would be
and I cherished you for it. Every time I looked at you my
heart would fill with love. And that's why I asked you to
marry me. And that's why I jumped like a clown when
you said yes. Now things would be perfect and everything
in life would start to make sense. And they did up to a
point. But you were concerned about your studies and
your career. I needed a woman I could be closer to and
more intimate with than you had time for, but I didn't
want to lose you either. That's when I met Louise. It
didn't start out as anything more than a one-night-stand
kind of thing that went on for more than a year when you
were out or too busy to be with me. Then one night
Louise threw a surprise at me. You remember that, don't
you, Louise? . . . It was your birthday, we were talking and
you told me you had a decision to make. You told me
about that other man you had been seeing and of the fact
that he had asked you to marry him. Then you asked me
what you should do. That's when I think I really fell in
love with you. The moment when you asked me that
question. You didn't try to pressure me or anything like
that. All you did was ask my advice. That's when it
occurred to me that if you married that man I would
never see you again. You would be locked up in his life

and gone out of mine forever. I couldn't face that, so I asked you to marry me, and you did.

You would think a man with two wives is rich enough and blessed enough. I did and I was. People ask how I did it and why didn't the women suspect. I worked as an auto parts salesman and was on the road all the time. Sometimes I'd be gone three weeks at a time. Plus the women lived in different towns. So it was easy. A phone call here, a present there covered a lot of absences.

Liquor, Las Vegas, Reno, Tahoe, Black Jack, and Keno I guess I could blame for my next marriage. That, and the fact that I was trying to support two households on one salary.

Marcy, I didn't mean to trick you or play with your feelings. What happened with us had to happen. God, fate, destiny, or whatever you want to call it brought us together that night. I was losing, you was losing, we both were drunk. At least high. Too high to make much sense of anything other than the fact that things couldn't be worse and here we were in never-never land where clocks and time don't mean a damn thing. You were the one who spoke to me first, if I remember right. You asked how things were going and I said, "Don't ask." I didn't even know your name and I don't think I looked at you. Then you said, "Let's pool our resources, maybe one of us can score." I pulled out what I had and you matched it with yours. Next thing I knew we were hitting jackpots and beating the dealers. One casino after another, the streak wouldn't stop. And people want to tell me there ain't no God. Remember all that money? I kissed you out of gratitude. That's how I think it got started. With a simple kiss. Then the judge was saying, "Do you take this woman," and I was saying, "I do." And I did too. Damn if I didn't.

Once is accident, twice is a mistake, three times is just stupidity, and four, well you need to be put in a cage. But I did what I did with my eyes wide open. And for a while I got to admit I felt like I was king of the hill. And if I coulda told it to any man I knew I think they would've envied me. Especially when they looked at Bea. In fact I know they used to envy me. Used to hate me too because I was the only one you had eyes for, Bea. And I should've said, "No." Should've run a thousand miles away. But I didn't. You were too sweet, too young, too beautiful, and too trusting. . . . That wedding night when you just laid there and said, "Teach me," I knowed I did the right thing in spite of the fact that I had already done the right thing three times before.

I had to be stopped because I would've continued. I know that now. This marriage business can get to be an addiction just as strong as cigarettes, liquor, or drugs. Especially if you are somebody who falls in love as strongly and deeply as I do.

Janet, Louise, Marcy, and Bea. I love you and I still do. Bea, you were the one who tracked me down and exposed me. You even managed to put a bullet in me, but I don't hate you. I don't hate any of you. That's why I asked to see you today. To tell you that.

The joke of it is, I'm talking to you behind this bullet-proof glass because they're afraid another one of you might try to do me some harm. . . . I'm going away where there won't be any women. And I'm going to be gone for a long, long time. But you know what? I'm never going to be alone. Tell you why. Because I'm going to be carrying each one of you right here (*Touches his head*) and whenever I need to I'll bring you back, sweet, warm and loving just the way it was when we were Mr. and Mrs. Husband and Wife.

Strange Encounter

Kadeem, a man in his early thirties

Alright . . . alright, this is how it fell out . . . I picked up this guy in this bar. I won't tell you where or who I was at the time. Enough to say he was, I was there and something drew us together. Fate, Kismet, vibes. Call it what you like. He asked if I wanted to dance and I said, "Sure." So we danced, and then we danced again. We talked, touched, and then he asked if I liked to walk. I said, "Sure." So we took a walk. We walked from one side of town to the other, holding hands all the way. Then he turned and said, "This is where I live. Want to come up and spend the night?" . . . I hesitated, trying to be cautious, I guess, then I said yes. We got upstairs, had a drink, then he told me he had a roommate. "He's in the other room," he said, "but he won't bother us unless you want him to." I told him, "No. You're enough for me, thank you." He smiled and said, "In that case, let's turn in."

Now I wasn't dreaming, but somehow it felt like I was. Because somewhere in the middle of the night I turned and realized that there was more than one other body in the bed with me. Unbeknownst to me his roommate had decided to join us, I guess. I didn't know this person. And of course you worry about all kinds of things in this era of plague we're living through. But even after all that sometimes you still wind up saying, "To hell with it. I'll go with the flow." Stupid, I know. Dangerous, you don't have to tell me. Nevertheless that's what I did. And those are the facts.

Morning arrived. I was alone in the bed. I could hear them in the kitchen talking and laughing. The radio or

TV was on, and I could even smell coffee brewing. I showered, dressed, combed my hair, and went out.

"Morning," I said. Nobody answered. The conversation stopped. The roommate was looking at the paper so I said: "What's the headline?" He didn't say anything. He just left the paper on the table, picked up his coffee, and went into his room.

"What's wrong with him?" I asked my friend. "I thought we had a good time last night." But he didn't answer either. He just stood there in his bathrobe sipping coffee.

"What's the matter?" I asked. Still I got no answer.

"Damnit, talk to me. What's going on? What the hell's the matter!"

Finally when I could take it no longer I went over and grabbed him by the collar. "Talk to me!" I insisted. "Don't treat me like this!" But before I could say more, I felt all the wind rush out of me. He had punched me in the gut and it was impossible to breathe. I just stood there frozen, gasping for breath.

I guess I must've fallen to the floor, but I don't remember it. All I recall is lying there with dozens of black spots moving around in front of my eyes. I looked around and I was alone again. My friend must've returned to his room. So I got myself to a standing position, made it to the door and then the elevator.

Outside a cab had just turned the corner, I waved it down and got myself home. The next three hours were spent in the bathtub trying to feel better, and wondering what the hell that was all about. . . . I did ultimately feel better, but I still haven't figured it out.

Black Is Black

Dave, mid forties, enters eating some KFC chicken and sipping a Coke. He sits and begins to talk.

You know, sometimes when you talk about the situation of being black in America, white people who don't know any better will tell you, you being oversensitive, suspicious, and egotistical. Some will even go so far as to say you're being paranoid. But they would have to get into a black man's skin one time and see how it is. Then they wouldn't say that anymore. Like, for example, every brother with any sense know, that if you ever get stopped by a cop—no matter for what stupid reason he stopping you—your best bet is to smile, answer the man "yessir" and "no, sir." And don't try to give him any smart talk when he starts pushing you around. Because all he's waiting for, is for you to look like you want to get hostile, because then he gon' try to bust your head open with his club or put a bullet in your kidney. And if it turn out you're innocent, then maybe plant some stuff on you and say it was a "drug bust." Who gon' doubt him? He is white and he's got the badge. You black and what do you have? Misery. Right? You go up in front of the judge you can cry "foul!" all you like. The man'll take one look at you and see you black. He know you guilty. So you wind up in the slams or in the hospital. Or maybe both. So, any way you look at it, you lose. That's how it is in America. And if I'm telling a lie, somebody shoot me. But, now every so often, every now and then, you see something happen that you don't believe. You seen it with your own two eyes. So, you can't deny it. But, you still don't believe it because it's so damn incredible, that's why.

I went to a boxing match not long ago. Madison Square Garden. Last big boxing event and everybody was there. Larry Holmes, Sugar Ray Leonard, Emile Griffith, Big George Foreman, Evander Holyfield and, the man himself, Mohammed Ali. You shoulda heard that crowd when Ali was introduced. Man, those people went wild. Tell you the truth, I don't even remember who was fighting that night. All I remember was all them celebrities. And, in a funny way, they was more important than the fight. Imagine, being under the same roof with all those famous people. All these people I had sometimes paid close to fifty or a hundred bucks just to see them do their stuff in the ring. Wow . . . everybody in the audience was happy he had chosen this night to come out and witness this thing. Then, the trouble start. The young black dude, who look to be somewhere in his mid twenties, was having a problem with the manager. He was sitting in a seat he claim he had a ticket for. But, the manager, this little bald white man said he had another person with a ticket for that same seat. "Show me your ticket," the manager called out. "I lost it," my man said. "Then you have to vacate." "Like hell, I will." You could see the manager was a little confused and didn't know what to do because other folks was encouraging that boy. "That's right, man. Don't let them push you around. Don't. Right! Right on!" And my man stood his ground. "You heard them. You want me out of this seat, you got to come in here and get me. And that's a fact!" Now, we all sitting there, knew his story was lame. If he really had a ticket, of course, he woulda showed it to the man but what these boys do is buy the cheap tickets, then sneak down to these expensive seats. That's what this boy musta done. But, now, the man caught him and he was putting on a show. But the manager didn't argue. He just said, "Excuse me," and left. But in a matter of minutes, he was back. This time with two cops in tow. White cops. "Show us your ticket stub." "I lost it," my man said spelling it out, "L-O-S-T I-T." "Then you got to leave," the cop told him. "Like hell I am. You want me outta this seat, you got to take me outta this seat." "You think it can't be done?" "Not by a little white faggot like you!" Now things was getting serious. This man was calling the cop names and you could see the cops wasn't liking it. . . . Some of us in the audience with some common sense was saying to the dude, "Hey man, be cool. You know how it is. They got the badge, they got the gun, and they got the color. You know you can't win, so give it up!" But, my man wasn't listening. He told them to take a flying you-know-what to the moon and leave him alone.

Finally, one cop said, "This is a waste of time." And push his way through the seats till he got to the boy. Well, when he got there, that boy didn't wait for change. Bam! He nailed the cop one up side his jaw! And when the cat was going down, caught him with the other hand in the ribs and then against his ear. It was a pretty thing to watch, and beautifully executed. But, of course, there was going to be hell to pay. You don't hit a cop in New York and get away with it. Hell no. Anybody with any street sense can tell you that. Now, one cop was down but the other cop was standing there big and tall with his gun pointed straight at my man. Some people try to duck out of the way, some people try to hide behind each other because we didn't want to get hit with no strays. And you never know about bullets. . . . But it didn't come to that. Because my man, when he saw the gun, came to his senses and went with the cops. "Well, that's the last we gon' see of him." "His ass is grass," somebody else said. We all took our seats shaking our heads because we know that in a matter of minutes, there was going to be one broken-up black boy. And that there was nothing in this world that anybody could do about it. There should be, but there wasn't. And that's just a simple fact of life.

Well, things settled down again and the main event

was just about to begin. Honestly speaking, I had all forgot about the boy and his problem because my interest was all caught up in the excitement of this thing. Then, I heard a noise in back. People clapping and cheering. When I turned around, I saw my man, the cat who had punched the cop, coming down the aisle, smiling and waving a ticket. He sat in his seat. The same seat he was in before they started hassling him. Well, you could've knocked me down with a feather. If you had bet me money that my man would've gotten away with knocking down a cop, you would've won all I had. To this day, I don't know how he worked it out. I saw it with my own eyes and to this moment, I still don't really believe it.

Where I Was, Where I Am

Dwyane, mid to late forties

I can remember exactly where I was and what I was doing when I first heard the news. But that isn't important. What is important I think was my attitude. I didn't pay it much mind. For me it wasn't like the day Kennedy was killed where everyone froze in their tracks, gathered in little groups and walked around like zombies for the rest of the day. No, it wasn't like that at all. Everyone was moving around, going about their business. I did too. See, nothing in the news report sounded definite. It was, "Our reporter on the scene said this . . . our other reporter said that . . . rumor has it that . . ." And the reports kept contradicting each other. The only thing known was the fact that King had been shot. No one knew if it was a serious or superficial wound, where the bullet came from or if anyone else was hurt. . . . There was talk of rushing him to the hospital, talk that it may not even be Martin who was shot. . . . Then the news came out definite and sure. "Martin Luther King, winner of the Nobel prize for peace, had been shot and killed by person or persons unknown." The story went on, but even then I didn't believe it. I'll tell you why. They'd said the same thing that time when that woman stabbed him with the letter opener or whatever it was she used, and it turned out not to be true. They had marked him off as dead, but he fooled them. He survived.

We have a habit in this country of giving things significance by elevating them to tragedy. The orgy we submerged ourselves into after the death of JFK was not to be believed. On radio, TV, or anywhere you looked on the street, somebody was there shamelessly exhibiting how miserable and grief stricken they were. . . . Now I happen to think that grief, sorrow, or whatever we want to call it is a private matter. Not something for us to put on display for all the world to see. I find it offensive. The spectacle of viewing someone in tears to me calls attention to the crier, and not the event they're supposedly crying about. When I think about it, it's more than offensive, it's obscene.

A nation would mourn, a nation would weep. And then this nation would go on as it did before.

We had been through this vulgar display once and I for one, didn't want for us to have to go through it again. "Oh God, no. Please no. Not again." . . . I was wishing and hoping against what I heard that the news report was wrong. I was hoping against hope that the reports of this particular shooting had been greatly exaggerated. But I was wrong. The reports were right and I was wrong. Simple as that, but not so simple. If it was I'd have forgotten it. I'd have gone on with my life. As it is, after all these years I'm still back there at the moment when I first heard the news. And I'm still wondering why it couldn't've been like I had fantasized. Like I had hoped. That "The reports of Mr. King's death had been greatly exaggerated."

A Memory

Arnie, a man in his late forties

In the movie *Citizen Kane*, the character Bernstein talks about a girl in a white dress with a parasol that he saw when crossing the ferry from New York to New Jersey. Their eyes met but they never spoke. Yet the memory of her haunted him every day of his life.

Well—I wasn't so lucky. We actually spoke, the young lady and I. It was one of those chance encounters that only happens a few times in anybody's life. I wandered into a coffee shop for breakfast, she came over to serve me, our eyes met, and we just begin to smile.

Being in my mid twenties at the time I lacked the arrogance I now have, so I just listened politely as she told me her name and asked if I lived in the area. Before I could get a chance to talk to her she was called away by the owner and his wife.

I looked around. There were only two other customers in the place. Both were at the counter sipping coffee and reading newspapers. Nobody needed her immediate attention, yet the owner and his wife pounced on her to get behind the counter. There was work to be done. Then, the owner's wife, a woman whose best days had been too many years ago, served my breakfast with a brisk efficient smile. When I was finished she served me more coffee and asked, "Will there be anything else?" All the while behind her I could see the waitress at the counter looking at me with a smile and what I determined was helplessness or apology in her eyes.

When I paid she glanced at me as if to say, "I'll be here

tomorrow." I nodded to let her know I understood and that I would be here too.

Outside I wondered why they didn't want me to talk to that girl. Or her to me. This was New York City in East Greenwich Village, so it couldn't be that other thing. In the Village you saw black and white couples together all the time.

"Well, there's always tomorrow," I said, echoing that great lady of the South: Scarlett O'Hara. "There's always tomorrow." . . . But it was a foolish dream. Because although tomorrow did arrive, she wasn't there. The place was, I was, even the time was the same. "Maybe she's off," I told myself. So I went back all that week and the week following that. She never showed up. Either she had quit or was fired. Whatever it was I never saw her again.

It's been nearly twenty years now and I still think about her and I still wonder, "What might have been." Bernstein in *Citizen Kane* was fiction, I am fact. Yet we both feel, I think the very same sense of loss. Isn't that odd?

Covey, the Slave Breaker

Character: Frederick Douglass—a man in his fifties, dressed in period garb, standing before a podium speaking to an audience.

It was a real profession in those days—*slave breaking*—and people did practice it. The man I was sent to, Edward Covey, was known as a first-rate "breaker." Captain Thomas' arrangement was that I should live with Mr. Covey for a year doing his bidding and learning to obey. For this, Mr. Covey would receive some small stipend and the benefit of all the work I would do on his farm.

(*Doing Covey's voice*) "You've been sent to me boy, because they say that you're difficult. I'm going to break you of those ways, I promise you that. As sure as the good Lord is above me. And since we have only a short time to achieve these results, I think we better get started right away."

With that he gave me three lashes and sent me to get wood from the forest with a yoke of unbroken oxen to draw the cart. Never having been around cattle before, I lost control of the beasts and made a mess of the job. For that I got three more lashes . . . For the next six months hardly a week went by that I wasn't striped at least once.

Covey was not a large man, but he was built quite compact. And had quick wiry motions. His face was narrow with small deep set eyes. Eyes that were always in motion. He spoke from the corner of his mouth in a sort of a growl. Nothing about this man made you comfortable in his presence.

And he seemed to be everywhere, lurking behind

bushes or crouched in a gully, ready to pounce. Bill Smith, another slave and I, when alone, never called him by any other name than "The Snake."

Although he liked to use the lash, Mr. Covey also thought that hard and continued labor was the best way to break a slave's spirit. So he steadily worked me to the limit of my strength. And would keep me at work in the field from dawn sometimes, until complete darkness. At certain seasons of the year we were all kept in the field until eleven or twelve o'clock at night.

It got so bad and I was so miserable that I often considered the possibility of suicide. But a mixture of hope and fear stopped me.

Now when I look back on that time of suffering it seems more a dream than a reality.

Covey had succeeded in breaking me. Rather than receive another swipe of the lash, or to simply escape another hour of work I would have gone anywhere, done anything, or be any kind of creature he bid me to be. But somehow Covey didn't seem to realize this, for he kept on applying more and more work and punishment.

One day in August 1834, I was hard at work in the yard with my two fellow slaves, Bill Smith, Bill Hughes, and a hired man named Eli. We were "treading" wheat. A simple task but one that requires strength and activity, rather than intelligence or skill.

I went to the stable. And was in the act of climbing to the loft when Covey jumped out of nowhere, his thin face set in a hard expression. He threw me to the floor and was trying to get a slipknot of rope around my feet. I evaded that, too.

He seemed so confident that he had me in his power, he didn't realize he was into a fight. For I had determined this man would beat me no longer. We stood equal before nature and he would find that out here and now.

"Are you resisting me?" he asked.

"Damn right, I am."

"Then I'm going to kill you boy."

He leapt at me and I kicked him hard in the stomach. He folded in two and was having trouble breathing. I could've struck him more and was tempted. But the laws in Maryland against such things were severe. I could've lost a limb or even my life. So I just walked out of the barn.

But Covey was determined. He leapt on me and we rolled into the yard. Again I was getting the better of him and was frustrating everything he tried to do to me. I wouldn't hit him but held him in such a way that he couldn't hit me. He struggled and stamped his feet, but I was holding him fast. At that moment one of the slaves, Bill Hughes, happened on the scene and Covey called to him.

"Bill! . . . Bill! . . . I want you over here."

(*As Bill, a caricature of a slow and sleepy black man*)

"Sah?"

"Come over here, goddamn you!"

"Yes . . . sure—anything you say."

"Take hold of this bastard. Get him off me."

(*Scratching his head*) "But Massa, I—got work to do, in the barn."

"This is your work. Take a hold of him now."

"No sir, I don't think so. Look more like your work to me. . . . And you having a damn hard time of it."

And with that Bill left. Covey struggled and struggled but I refused to let him go.

"You intend to keep me here all day?"

"No. But if you try to whip me, I'm going to try to kill you. You whipped me enough and ain't gon' ever whip me no more. I swear that to the God in heaven above us."

"Let me go!" he gasped one more time and I did.

(*Pause*)

We looked at each other, panting like two animals.

"Now you scoundrel, back to work," he said. "I

wouldn't have whipped you so hard if you hadn't attempted to fight back."

In its way it was amusing, the man hadn't touched me. If anything it was I who had inflicted some pain. But he needed to say that in order to save face.

There was no dignity in this battle with Mr. Covey. But for the following months I continued living on his farm the man never laid his hand on me again. And, to the best of my knowledge, he never said anything about it to anyone. I suspect he was ashamed to let people know that he had been bested by a sixteen-year-old boy. It certainly would've compromised his reputation as a first-rate overseer and Negro breaker.

A Garden in the City

A man over fifty comes out with some potted plants, goes back to get a couple more. He also has some gardening tools and maybe a watering can. He's dressed for his chores, complete with an old straw hat to shield his face from the sun. It is a summer day. He sits on a stool and works with the plants for a while.

People hear about Harlem and they think it's just an area where violence and death is a twenty-four-hour, round-the-clock occurrence. Well, that's silly, isn't it? People live here, of course. And these people call this place their home. Me, I ain't never been anywhere else. And for a lot of folks I know the situation is the same.

Walking along a Hundred Thirty-ninth the other day, I got to talking to a woman I ain't never seen before. How that even happen is interesting. I was going to the Superette when this woman pluck my sleeve and say to me, "Young man, I'll give you a dollar if you give me a hand." Well, I had to look at her. Anybody who call me young at this age deserve a second look. So I stop and could see the woman was older. She was carrying two shopping bags full of stuff. And I could see they was straining her. "I'll help you, Mama," I said, and we started walking. She lived only a block and a half away. As we walked we talked about the neighborhood and all the changes we'd seen over the years. "I've seen so many changes, I can't remember the half of them," she said. "Me, too," I told her.

"You're a young man, I'm talking about real change," she said. I told her I'd lived in Harlem most of my life and had to have seen every change she say. Especially in this neighborhood.

"How old do you think I am?" she asked. I looked at her close. She wasn't young, so I guessed about eighty.

"I'm a hundred and four," she said, and I got to tell you, it took my breath away. . . . Because as I looked at her again I could see her face was all wrinkles and there was a lot of hair grown out of her cheek and stuff. Also her ears look big. And that's something that happens when people start getting real old. Their ears get big.

"A hundred and four," I said again.

"Yeah," she said, "one oh four and in all them years I ain't moved more than six blocks in either direction."

"You got any family?"

"All passed on. I'm the last of six girls and close to thirty grandchildren. I outlive everybody."

"How are you feeling?"

"Feel fine. Feel I could go another fifty or sixty years maybe."

We got to her building and some boys she knew ran over and took the bags from me. She insisted that I take the dollar for helping her, so I did. One of the boys got the door while the other helped her in. Clearly the people in that building treated her like some kind of treasure. And she was.

After she left I just stood there thinking about all the history that has passed through that woman. Everything from the Reconstruction period to the Martin Luther King bus boycott. From the Wright Brothers getting their plane off the ground to the men landing on the moon. And in all that time she had never moved more than six blocks in any direction. "Feeling fine. Feel I could go another fifty or sixty years maybe." . . . Ain't that something, though?

(*Pause. He goes back to his plants, gets a new thought*) There's a man down the street. Retired too. Used to be a cop on the beat for nearly thirty years. Didn't live here.

Just worked here. But kept the same patrol all that time. Wasn't a nice cop or a kind man. Matter of fact if he was anything he was a skunk and a dog. Took advantage of his authority. Push people around. And for years on end had the whole neighborhood afraid of him. Word had it that one night somebody was going to creep up behind him with a bat and bust his head open. But nobody ever did. Then . . . much to all our surprise, when that man retired this is where he come to live. This neighborhood, where as far as anybody know, he didn't have a friend. . . . He's been here about eight years now. People still talk behind his back about what a low dog he used to be. But they now play dominoes with him, invite him to parties and church socials. And discuss the news of the day when they pass him on the stoop. I guess he's so old, ain't no point carrying a grudge no more. So now he's one of us.

(*Brief pause as he takes care of his plants*) I'm retired, too. They call me the Flower Man. Actually, I don't grow too many flowers. One or two over there. But mostly it's vegetables, greens and a little bit of corn. Things people can put in their pot and eat. Almost everything I eat these days come from right here. But people started calling me "The Flower Man" and the name stuck.

I didn't start out being a gardener. This hobby came to me late in life. When I worked, I was a traffic manager for a company in Long Island. Held the same job for over twenty-seven years. My wife, Claudette, was a cook but she worked for the phone company most of her years till she got sick and passed on. Never had any kids, but got a few nephews who come by to see me from time to time.

This gardening thing started out . . . I don't know. They knocked the building down and the lot was sitting empty. People was throwing garbage and stuff here, smelling up the neighborhood. So a group of us one weekend decide to clean up the mess and petition the city for permission to plant here. Well, the city said they had plans for putting up some kind of community center. But we could use it as a garden till they was ready. That was eleven years ago.

Bunch of us marked off sections and began to plant things. I had never done anything like that before so I was just following the others. After a while I bought a couple of books, read up on gardening, and things start to grow. Folks say I have a natural green thumb. I don't know. I just know that since I retired this is where I spend most of my days, winter or summer.

People say you should talk to plants. I ain't starting to do that yet. I ain't crazy. But I do think of them as my non-human friends so I got to come by and see how they doing. See if they need anything.

I don't sell what I grow here either. I like to give it away. Sometimes people leave a donation so I can buy more seeds, fertilizer and stuff like that.

These days I have the biggest section to grow in. And they even have a little copper sign that say, "Lester's garden where magic food grow." It was put up on my birthday last year. We even had a little party on the walk.

One of these days, the city gon' put a building over this spot. But until then we gon' let the ground keep giving us its blessing.

So—when you hearing all that stuff about Harlem, remember all the things that they don't put in the paper. Like the fine people who live here. And places like this garden in the middle of all this concrete.

Lights fade as he returns to his plants and begins to take them away, mumbling softly.

Don't tell anybody I'm talking to you. But you girls looking fine. Getting a whole lot of sun. And showing your leaves real pretty. Keep up the good work, hear?

LIFETIMES ON THE STREETS

Production Notes
The Cast
In an evening such as this the cast size varies according to the resources of the producing organization and the versatility of the actors. Ideally, each actor/actress should do two or more monologues, with the exception of the actors playing Mavis and the Derelict only doing those roles.

The saxophone man may or may not play the instrument. Since he is always behind the scrim he could just mime the movements to recorded music.

In addition to the roles of *Mavis* and the *Derelict*, types required are as follows:

> *Black Woman,* mid to late twenties
> *Black Man,* early to mid thirties
> *Black Man,* fifties
> *Black Woman,* thirties

The Setting
There should be essentially a bare stage with a few chosen items (a wire garbage can, a bus stop sign, a neon bar sign, maybe a porn movie poster, etc.) to suggest the urban setting of the play.

Some productions have utilized slides depicting scenes and images of black life (particularly Harlem) along with shots of some of the people mentioned (Lena Horne, Fats Waller, Malcolm X). Also in back might be a scrim where ghostly evocations of people or times remembered can be seen. Again this is up to the resources of the producing organization.

Note: The stage setting for *Act Two* should be altered somewhat from the setting of *Act One.* Perhaps the positions of the benches could be changed. More posters could be added. And maybe a different neon sign from a different angle can be seen.

Characters wander out, get caught in a light, stop, and tell their story to the audience, moving about, using the whole space sometimes. Other times holding ground in one area.

When finished one character may leave the stage as another enters. Or move to another spot and become part of the setting. (This is left to the discretion of the director.)

In some productions all members of the cast except Mavis and the Derelict are kept on stage throughout the show. They stand, sit, or move about, reading newspapers, drinking sodas, tending babies, and so forth. When it's their turn to speak they move forward or talk to other cast members who never respond.

Music and other sound effects indicated in the text may be used throughout. Or perhaps other sounds of the city streets (sirens, horns, car tires skidding) may be incorporated.

ACT ONE

Prologue

Over black a voice is heard. It could be male or female.

We are the invisible people. The faces without names. We live all over America but are never identified or acknowledged unless we start a riot or commit a crime. Our struggles are considered insignificant and our joys are viewed as trivial. Yet we persevere. Only here in Harlem are we not seen as statistics but as flesh-and-blood beings with loves . . . hopes . . . dreams . . . and desires.

Lifetimes on the Streets: monologues and vignettes on black life. The stories behind some of the faces we see but never get to know.

The sound of someone playing a saxophone is heard as the lights come up to begin Act One.

Note: In some productions, slides depicting scenes and images of urban black life were shown on a screen while the prologue was being said, or the words of the prologue were seen on a screen while being heard over the speakers.

Mavis #1

We see a man behind the scrim playing on a saxophone. Neon lights of the city are reflecting off him as he plays something improvisational and bluesy.

A spotlight discovers Mavis somewhere off the side of the stage. She comes forward. She speaks with a West Indian accent.

I never used to like this place. Only reason I ever come up here was to get my hair done. Used to be a beauty parlor 'round the corner on Courtland Avenue. Prices was good and a woman there, Miss Bertha, knowed how to do my hair just right. She was the one who did my hair when I got married. At that time I was living in the Bronx. But even when we moved to Brooklyn I still continue going to her. Not all the time, you know. Just when it was something special. Christmas or Easter, a christening or maybe my birthday.

I'm from Jamaica. Been living in this country since I was a little girl. But I ain't comfortable with people from New York. I don't know why. But at Miss Bertha's I used to always feel at home. I don't know why that is either.

Anyhow it was a winter day when I come looking for the beauty shop. Miss Bertha's Beauty Shop. My sister was coming from Florida and I wanted to look good for she and her husband. So I took the afternoon off from work to come get my hair done. But when I got to the place everything was gone. The sign, the business, the whole thing. Gone. It was like Miss Bertha never was there. The building was all barred up. Nobody was there. I couldn't believe it. So I walked 'round the corner and asked the first man I meet what happened to Miss Bertha's? He didn't know so I said "Excuse me," and the man went on.

It was close to six months since the last time I had been there. Boy, the world sure change in a short while. Miss Bertha musta moved somewhere but there wasn't a sign or nothing. I didn't know what to do. So I just walked around the area looking and looking. Three times I run into the same man I asked the first question to. The fourth time he said, "Still looking for that place?" I told him, "Yes." And told him I was puzzled. He said to me, "It's cold and you look like you could use a cup of tea." I told him he was right. So we went into a coffee shop but I told him I could pay for mine.

He couldn't a been more than twenty-seven or twenty-eight. A boy, next to me, although I'm only thirty-eight. In conversation I asked what kind of work he do. He told me, "Nothing. Just paint." "Paint like what?" I ask. He smile. "Anything," he say. "But mostly I like to paint people."

He didn't look shabby, but I got the feeling he didn't have much money, so I offered to pay for the tea. "In that case then I have to buy you dinner," he said. I ask him why but he didn't answer. He just smiled. "I have to go home," I told him. It was already getting late. But somehow the way he smile and didn't try to push made me say yes.

We sat in this little dark place, this restaurant, and he ordered some kind of wine. Next thing I knew he was opening the door, showing me where he lived. It was cold and there was a lot of half-finished paintings around. The room was so cold that even when he made coffee it wasn't enough to really make me warm. So we got into this mattress he had lying in a corner. Pull the blanket up over us and begin to nestle-up close. I don't remember much about the night except that I was dizzy and his arms around me felt warm and cozy.

Next morning he walked me to the train and I told him good-bye. On the ride all the way back to Brooklyn I found myself wondering why I had done it and what I would tell my husband. I had never done anything like that before. And you know, it's funny. I didn't regret it. As I rode the train I was smiling. And smiling and smiling. And smiling.

Lights fade as the sax player continues. A flash of lightening followed by a crack of thunder signals the light change.

New Ice Age #1

A Derelict wearing a tattered old raincoat carries a duffel bag. He is a man past fifty, but seems ageless.

Would you look at the sky. Listen to that noise. Damn. You can even see the clouds turning cold. Wintertime here in Harlem. Ain't no other place like it. People rushing from the subway stations trying to get home. Oriental-Korean folk turning on the lights on their fruit stands then going back to hide behind the glass. Seem to me only a short while ago we was at war with them people. Now they taking over the area and ain't nobody saying a damn thing about it. The march of time, I suppose. Don't nothing remain the same. Everything changes. Everything, I guess, except me. I remember, for example, how there used to be a string of barbershops all along the boulevard here. Anytime a night or day you want some news of what was happening in the area. Or maybe you just want a place to hang out and chew the fat. That's where you went. Into one a them barbershops . . . Now that too is gone. Today you want a haircut, got to make an appointment. Imagine that? An appointment to get your hair cut. Then the man got to know you else he won't push the buzzer to let you through the front door. Everybody is suspicious. Everybody is afraid. Crime is everywhere these days. Dope making fools feel good. Liquor keeping the rest of us sane.

Stops. Takes a bottle from his pocket and drinks from it.

Yeah. When it's cold outside you want to be warm inside. That's common sense . . . Only thing is, it feel to me like these streets is getting colder. And the winters getting longer. I'm beginning to think we going through a new ice age where everything gon' wind up frozen cold and dead if we ain't careful. That's why I got to hold unto this thing, (*Raising his bottle*) to keep me from freezing. (*He takes another sip*)

Want some? (*He offers it to the audience*) No? You don't know what you're missing.

Pause. Behind the scrim a woman and man in 1940s clothes can be seen laughing and dancing to music heard in the distance.

Reefers, alcohol, hot music, and folks laughing. That was a time when Harlem was paradise. And I remember it so well. All the gods was in their kingdom. Louis, Billie, Ethel, Fats, Duke, Bo, Lena, Bessie, Cab, and Dinah . . . Damn. Makes my heart smile just to hear myself saying those names.

Magic, magic, magic times they were. Ladies in tuxedo dresses with pressed hair. Me, narrow and light, hip to all the new sliding dances.

The sound of the music comes up and he moves into a few dance steps, then stops.

Now I'm sorry to say it's gone. All gone.

But, hey. I ain't ashamed to say I knew a lot of women. Knew a lot a wild boys, too. Some died on the streets. A lot went away. But I stayed. Yeah, I stayed. Know why? . . . Didn't have no place to go, I guess.

But that wasn't the only reason. I didn't want to go. Plus somebody had to stay and bear witness. Know what I mean? Somebody had to stay to tell the young people how it used to be. The kind of people and magic that used to be on these streets. Funny thing is, the young people don't want to know. They just ain't interested. But they should be. (*Shouting*) YOU! and YOU! and YOU! LISTEN UP AND HEAR ME. YOU ALL WALKING ON HALLOWED GROUND. THESE STREETS WAS BLESSED WITH THE MUSIC OF OUR SOULS. GOSPEL . . . JAZZ . . . BLUES AND ALL THE OTHER SOUNDS IN-BETWEEN. MUSIC FROM OUR JOYS AND OUR FEARS. MUSIC THAT WAS THE CRY OF OUR SPIRITS. YOU DON'T WANT TO HEAR, BUT I'M TELLING YOU THE TRUTH.

More cracks of thunder and flashes of lightning.

Oh, Lord, it's getting colder. Feel that wind? Even alley cats don't want to be out on a night like this. Got to find me a place to keep these old bones warm. New ice age is definitely coming on us. I can feel it. Got to hibernate till all this bad weather pass. Then the sun will come out again, I hope. But all the while I'm hibernating I'll have this [*his bottle*] and all my memories to keep me warm. Let me ask you a question. What will you have?

He exits and the lights change. Music accompanies the change as the stage becomes washed in a blue light.

Delores

Delores, a hooker, comes out. She is an attractive woman in her mid thirties wearing tight, revealing clothes. She smokes all the while.

Oh please, don't be asking me how I come to be doing this kinda stuff for a living. First of all it ain't no goddamn body's business. Second, what I do with my body is my affair. You don't see me going around asking all them middle-class housewives if they love them husbands they spending every night with or if they doing it just for a promising future.

'Nother thing I want to ask all them folks who want to tell me about morality is: Where are you when I need money for food and clothes? Or when the Super knocking at my door telling me to pay the rent or get the hell off a his premises. Don't nobody jump up and say 'Hey, baby, here's a few dollars to keep the wind and snow off of your back.' Hell no. All any man ever want to do is buy you ten drinks and slide their hands under your dress. So why the hell not make them pay for it and whatever else they get afterwards too. Hell, it pays the rent and keep me from taking a knife or razor and cutting some dude for the spare change he got in his pocket.

And don't believe I would find that too hard. Wouldn't bother me at all. I could do it just like that. (*Snaps her fingers*)

'Cause you see, I don't like you people. Don't like none a you at all. You ain't ever treat me nice and ain't no reason for me to treat you all any better.

First real boyfriend I ever had used to put crushed up

aspirin in my drinks 'cause he thought it would make it easier for him to do whatever it was he wanted to do to me later on. And then when I let him that lover took pictures. Polaroid pictures and showed it to his friends. Might've even sold a few. I don't know.

My next man was white and his mother told him to have nothing to do with me 'cause I was black and not up to his standard. He told me his mother was a bigot and a pig. But he kept coming to my house. Only thing is it was always after one o'clock in the morning when nobody was out on the street. And he always left around six before anybody serious was up to see him leaving. Then one day he called to tell me he wouldn't be seeing me no more 'cause he was getting married and had to change his ways.

Damn, I loved that man. I don't know why but I did. I didn't even care that I couldn't see him except late at night. Told myself it wasn't his fault that we live in the kind of world we live in. Those few hours laying next to each other in that dark warm bed were some of the happiest times I think I ever had. And hey, I ain't had that much happiness in my life that I could afford to throw any little bit away.

I got me some kids. (*Pause*) Looking at me you wouldn't believe that, would you? Two boys and a girl. I don't know where they is. And don't want to know either. Their father was a photographer and we was legally married. I was sixteen and a half, he was twenty-four. People used to say I was pretty. Even my mother used to say it. But she used to also like to add that "Prettiness don't last forever." Maybe that's why she push me into marrying Les even though it was clear that I was too young—and he was too old.

I had three children in two and a half years. And woulda had more if he didn't start cheating and staying out nights and sometimes weeks at a time. Then when I proceeded to do the same thing that man beat the hell outta me and told people I was a whore.

When I spoke to my mother about it she told me that sometimes marriage can be a heavy cross to bear. When I said I wanted to come home she said she didn't have no room in her house.

So I ran off with his best friend who promised he would marry me soon as I got my divorce. Instead he just moved out one night while I was at work. People say he was shacking up with a woman named Angie who lived across the way. But when I went to visit her—she was gone, too. "Moved and left no forwarding address," was the message.

Court cited me for abandonment and declared that I was an unfit mother. His parents took the three kids. Hell, that wasn't no surprise. Ever since those kids was born those folks started taking them over. This was just a technicality. What was I supposed to do? Fight City Hall?

I been beat. I been used. I been worked over. Can't remember a man ever using the word "love" to me except as a way of taking some kind of advantage. Hell, what I do now is honest. More honest than all the other stuff I used to do when people used to say I was respectable. So I don't see no disgrace in it. I don't see no shame. I am a woman. My kind of woman doing what I can to make my way through life. You don't like the way I am . . . tough.

She blows smoke at the audience and leaves. Lights change.

Sorry to Disturb You

A man in his mid thirties appears, speaking very fast.

Excuse me, ladies and gentlemen. I don't mean to upset your fine sunny morning but the condition I find myself in leave me no other choice . . . As you can see from the way I'm dressed I'm not a derelict or a bum. I'm in worse shape than that . . . You see . . . You see . . . I—I—have Acquired Immune Deficiency Syndrome. AIDS. That's right, I have AIDS! M-m-m-my problem is that—that I—I don't don't—don't—er—(*He exhales audibly*)

My problem is that I don't know how I got it. I'm not a homosexual, intravenous drug user or member of any third world population. I've never had a blood transfusion, consorted with prostitutes or ever indulged in offbeat sex of any kind. For all intents and purposes, so far as those things are concerned, my life has been blameless. Yet I was diagnosed as having AIDS.

And I know the diagnosis is correct because I've been sick. And my physical condition seem to deteriorate sometimes by the hour. Other times, such as today I feel fine. Even hopeful.

The last thing I want to do is stand here and beg you for money. It's something I never thought I'd ever be doing in my life. But life deals us funny cards sometimes. And I hope the one I got is never passed on to you.

(*Another breath*)

I was a carpenter working on a construction site when I first started feeling sickly and strange. But I didn't pay it any mind. I took some Excedrins and it went away. Two days later it came back again. This time it didn't go away.

So I went to one doctor, then a second and then a third. They didn't know what was wrong with me. One suggested a long rest and a change in my dietary habits.

Somewhere along the way my test slides were sent to a veterinary hospital on a hunch from my last doctor. His instinct turned out to be right. What I had was a rare kind of pneumonia that usually only attacks parakeets. The human system repels the disease when it strikes. But because I have AIDS that defense was broken down and I became infected.

I'm telling you all this not so much to solicit your sympathy as your understanding.

I'm unemployed because I can't hold a hammer for any length of time. Or saw a straight line through lumber. I've been to every agency the city has for people like me. Some have given help for a day or two. But nothing on a continuous basis. I'm not gay, so the doors of those support groups aren't open to me.

Three months ago I was evicted from my apartment because I couldn't pay the rent. Every friend I have doesn't seem to want to see me. They treat me as though I'm already dead. My problem is, I'M STILL ALIVE.

I can't work so I have no income. Welfare will only take you so far then you're cut off and sent from social service office to social service office only to be told you don't fit into their guidelines.

I live in a flophouse whenever I get the money. They're not expensive. So most days just from what I get from begging I can sleep with a roof over my head.

(*Pause again*)

I'm going to sing when I pass the hat. Don't mind me, it's just something I have to do. . . . I never used to be religious. I never used to be much of anything. I guess when the end starts getting near you start thinking about all kinds of possibilities.

Because I have no family, you and the rest of the world

becomes my kin. Please help me if you have the means.
And if you don't just offer me your good wishes—I'll take
anything I can get. God bless you all.

*He begins singing "Jesus Loves Me" as he moves through the
audience shaking his hat which already contains a few coins.
Lights change. Behind the scrim we see a man playing the saxophone while a woman moves sensuously to the music.*

Mavis #2

Mavis comes out, looks at them for a while, then begins to talk to the audience.

It was the same dream for—I don't know how many weeks in a row. The man would be sitting in this big empty room without any clothes on playing on this saxophone. Just playing and playing. Not for anybody. Just for himself. But he playing music like it coming from the inside of his bones. The kind of music you keep hearing all day when you sitting at your desk at work. Or going to the grocery. Or just looking at all your friends, thinking 'bout their lives. And then thinking 'bout your own.

The man plays, the woman dances some more.

In the dream the man is alone. But then there's a woman with him. She is kinda like dancing around while he playing. She's naked, too. And the room is full of light. He's playing and she's dancing around. . . . Sometimes it seems like I is that woman. But I know I ain't because I'm standing or sitting somewhere looking at her in this room. But in a funny way I know what she feeling. I can feel what she feeling as that man continue playing that music cause the music is like fingers. Fingers on this soft hand. Touching you all over. These warm soft hands touching you and touching you everywhere. And it feel good. Ohhh soooo good. And you want it to last forever. But it don't. The dream always end before anything real could begin to happen. The man and I sit on the bed looking at each other. Sometimes we even talk. But before I could touch

him or anything could get real something always interfere.
(*Pause*)

Russell is strange in his own way. I go up there to see him but I never know if he happy or not to see me. Or if he just doing it to pass the time away. Whenever I try to talk about feelings, he always say "Why do we have to put everything into words?" I'm not clear on what he mean, but I just sense that he don't like to talk, so I don't. I just lie there and enjoy it. And when it's over I go home again to my husband who don't seem to care that I been away for all that time.

Ain't No Other City Like It

Andy, a man in his forties, appears. He starts out laughing.

Saw a thing on the street I got to tell you about. Damn if this city ain't the craziest place. New York, New York. This place so nice they had to name it twice. New York, New York, center of the universe. They come from every corner of the earth, just to say they walked these streets once. Me, I was born, raised, and bred here. Oh, I've been away, seen a few places, but I got to tell you. Ain't no place like the Big Apple. Don't no other place even come close. You got rot, you got filth, you got evil, you got urban decay and you got greed. Alongside that you got wealth, pace, luxury, decadence, religion, despair, violence, and hope. I seen people die on the streets. But I also assisted a woman who was having a baby in a subway station. They come and they go but the parade never end.

Tell you what I mean:

One night I was going home from work when I passed these two girls walking and giggling on the sidewalk. One of them called out and said, "Hi there, Andy." I couldn't think of what girl I knew around that age so I went back to investigate. "You know me?" I asked. The girl turned and start to laugh, "See you don't even recognize your friends," one of them said. When I look a little closer the girl turned out to be a boy who work in the Superette round the corner from me. He was dressed up with wig and make-up and everything I wouldn'ta knowed who it was if he didn't tell me. After he left I kinda got to thinking. Now suppose I was a sailor out on leave looking for some action and I pick up this boy thinking it was a girl.

See how a boy could get himself beat up, killed maybe. Children come in this world and they don't even know their own danger. And in the world we live in now—you can't even tell the boys from the girls. That's how crazy things is here in the Big Apple.

Tell you another:

On the street corner near Sixth Avenue used to be a balloon man every night, selling balloons with little paper legs on them. He claim they dance and wiggle by themselves. But me and my friend Freddy know he got them hooked on a string that another cat standing ten feet away tugging with his finger. Freddy and me used to watch him sell that stuff to the tourists and laugh. It was a simple con that wasn't harming nobody. Got so the cat even knew us and used to say, "Hey there, my friends." And we would warn him when the cops was coming so he could pack up his stuff and move to another corner quick. Things went on like that for about a year. Then—

One Friday night Freddy and I on our way to the movies saw a crowd up by the balloon seller's corner. We went over to look and saw him lying on the pavement with his chest covered in blood. Somebody had shot him but his eyes was open and flickering. I told him to "Take it easy man. Help is coming." He look up at me and I think he mighta smiled. By the time the cop car got there, he was gone. Dead to the world and the noise of that street. I never did find out who shot him or why. But I got to say, we was sorry to see him go. Now when I pass that corner just don't seem the same. But I'll never forget him. He is somebody whose memory will always stay with me.

But that—that ain't what I meant to tell you about. What I stopped to say was about something I seen just a while ago . . . I was walking the street on my way to the train when I pass this white cat standing on the corner talking to this little crowd about Jesus. He had a microphone and some little portable speaker so I could hear

everything he was saying clear. Thing that got my attention was the cat was white, and Southern. I could tell that
by his accent. But all the people listening to him was
black. Wasn't that many but they was paying close attention, and every time he'd say, "Jesus is our master! Jesus is
our lord! Without him can't none of us be saved!" them
brothers and sisters would answer, "Yessir," "Amen!" "Talk
it like it is!" "Tell it plain!" and stuff like that. And my
man, the more they call to him the more excited he would
get. "And Jesus is the man! Jesus is our only hope for our
salvation on this planet. Jesus is the one who sees all,
knows all and who'll treat us with compassion. Jesus who
died for our sins and rose again. Jesus who walked on
water and told Peter not to doubt. Jesus who turned water
into wine. Jesus who said, 'Get thee behind me Satan.'
Jesus who is a faggot like I am. That's right, I said Jesus
who is a faggot, like I am asks you to understand all men
and love them as your brothers. Jesus who said, 'When you
harm the lowliest of my creatures, you also harm me.'" . . .

Well, when he said that thing about Jesus being a faggot, I guess it made an impression on this one big brother
who was standing there shouting "Amen." Because he went
over to that Southerner and said, "Take that back about
Jesus being a faggot. Jesus wasn't no homo and I ain't listening to nobody saying that."

But the Southerner wouldn't stop. He just kept saying,
"Jesus is a homo like I am and there ain't nothing wrong
with it. No sir, brothers and sisters, ain't nothing wrong
with it!" Well—he musta said it about three times when
that big brother took his fist and punch the cat BAM! in
his mouth. Preacherman went down and the big brother
stood over him. "I's about to stomp you if you don't take
that back about Jesus." The Southerner looked around for
help, but wasn't nobody coming forward. And wasn't no
cop in sight. Matter of fact instead a helping there was cats
shouting, "Stomp the Peckerwood, my man. Let's see his

tongue and his eyes bulge out." So the brother raised his foot. But before he could bring it down the Southerner said, "I'm sorry. I'm sorry. I made a mistake. Jesus was no fag. I take it back." "You sure? You positive?" the big brother asked. "Yes. It was a stupid thing for me to say. A dumb thing to say. And I take it back. I take it all back."

The brother looked down and I guess he felt the Southern man was talking straight because he reached down and helped him up, dust his coat off, and helped him to find his mike. After that the brother went back to the group he was standing with. When I left the Southern man was talking about Jesus, and the black folks including my man was shouting "Amen!" . . . Now ain't that a trip? Every corner you cross got something like that going on. If it ain't a preacher it's a whore and her pimp or a mother and her son. Or a man and his old lady. Twenty-four hours a day, seven days a week. I tell you man, only in this city. Only in NYC. Hey, I gotta run. Catch you again soon. . . .

He exits.

Stop Me If You've Heard This

The stage goes black and a spotlight reveals a young black woman in her early thirties. She comes out, composes herself, then begins.

Alright, here goes. (*To the audience*) Stop me if you've heard this. "Three fine black brothers riding in a private plane crash on this desert island. One brother died and after the first week they decided to bury him because they were embarrassed at what they were doing to his body. Then after the second week they dig him up again because they were embarrassed at what they were doing with each other."

(*Pause for a laugh. None comes. She starts again*)

Maybe I'm doing it wrong. You see, there was these three fine black brothers.

(*A baby from another room starts crying*)

Take it easy, honey, Mommy's trying to find a way to make a living. Alright, let's try this one. "How many feminists does it take to unscrew a light bulb?"

(*Baby continues crying*) Damn, why you got to cry so much? Seem to me like from the minute you open your eyes and look at the world all you can think to do is cry. Is there that much misery in this place that you can't find nothing to laugh about even when I tickle your little cute belly? . . . I know things ain't been the best but the day you give up hope is the day you really start to lose. . . .When me and your daddy had you the sun was shining bright and the city was a happy place. He said we would bring you up in our image and likeness. And that's what I'm trying to do, baby. Trying to keep the dream. But you got to help me. You got to stop crying so much. You got to smile once in a while. You got to make me think the world is the happy sunny place I once thought it was.

Your daddy ain't here no more. So it's you and me alone, baby. You and me alone. He woulda been here if he could. But that cop took that out of his hands. Black cop too. Didn't have no reason to pull his pistol and fire like that. Shoulda stopped to get the facts first. But somebody called out "Thief!" and a young black boy took off running in a crowd. Danny turned the corner coming from the subway station. As the boy ran past him, bullet hit Danny square in the chest as the thief made his escape. They say Danny looked so surprised as he lay on that sidewalk dying. And all he kept saying to the people around is "What happened? What happened?" Cop admit he overreacted and he was suspended from the force. Now they got a psychiatrist saying he was under a lot of stress and that shooting wasn't really his fault. "Just an accident," they say. "Just a tragic accident." All of that is fine but it don't bring back my husband or your daddy. Everybody say I gon' get a nice chunk of money out of this once the city and the lawyers get finished with the court and the papers. IS THAT REALLY WHAT THEY THINK I WANT? DO THEY REALLY THINK I'M SO POOR THAT I WOULD TRADE IN A HEALTHY LOVING HUSBAND FOR ALL THE MONEY THIS CITY HAVE TO GIVE?

I WANT MY HUSBAND BACK!
I WANT MY HUSBAND BACK!
I WANT MY HUSBAND BACK!
I WANT MY HUSBAND BACK!

(*Composing herself*) No. I can't go on like this. Got to keep the dream. Got to keep my sanity.

Stop me if you heard this one. . . . In the window of a butcher shop there is a sign. White brains, ten dollars a pound. Black brains, ten dollars a pound. Spanish brains, ten dollars a pound. Policeman's brains, three hundred dollars a pound. So this man walk into the shop and ask: "Why does it cost so much to buy a pound of policeman's brain?" The butcher looks at him and says, "Do you know how many cops you have to kill to get a pound of brain?"

(*Pauses again*) No, I guess I did that one wrong, too. Let's try it again. (*Takes a breath*) Alright, here goes—(*The baby starts crying again*)

Dammit, honey. Alright, I'll pick you up. But you got to stop this crying. Mommy got to get this right. 'Cause if she don't, how she going to earn a living?

She exits.

Women! Women! Women!

The stage fills with light. Ben, a man in his mid thirties, comes out.

Women, women, women. Wow! They are everywhere, ain't they though? Damn! Look in that direction, walk that way, hang out on this street corner here and you can't help but run into one, run into ten. Run into hundreds. That's how it is in this damn town.

Only problem is everyone is busy. Every woman I see got her eyes fixed on something or somebody that ain't me. Always the guy over there or the girlfriend over here, but not me.

How do you meet one a these foxy ladies, talk to her, maybe get a date? I don't know. Everybody is moving too fast and in too much of a hurry. You want to say, "Whoa Momma hold up, pause . . . wait for a minute." But you can't. Or if you do the woman'll just look at you like you a bug and just keep going.

It's a big problem. How does me a single man meet an interesting woman in a city as big and as busy as this one.

One cat I knew used his dog as a means of meeting the ladies. He used to walk this dog, a poodle, four, five time a day. It worked, too. Women would go up to the dog, talk to it, pet it, and my man Charlie would make his move. He told me he was meeting five, six women a week just with that dog. Only problem was, the dog didn't last. The poor thing was so exhausted from all them daily walks that one day it just lay down and didn't get up again. Now Charlie's trying to find another dog.

I must be sick because I look around and I want them

all. The secretaries, the policewomen, students, housewives, models, travel agents, salesgirls, architects, schoolteachers, waitresses, athletes, bank clerks, government workers, nurses, news reporters, singers, mail carriers, booksellers and all the others in between. I'm a shallow person. I know it and I admit it. My last girlfriend said I was sad because all I ever think about is sex. But that ain't true. I think about other things too. Like money, career, politics, family, friends, TV, outer space, money again, and sometimes even death. But I got to admit I think about sex a lot.

Now famous people look to have it the easiest. Or that's the way I see it. I mean if I was famous all I'd have to do is walk up to any chick and say "Hi, baby." She'd look at me, recognize who I was and say "Hi" back with a big inviting smile. After that it would be just a matter of letting nature take its course. Ain't that so?

Now I hear people say famous folks have it just as tough as the rest of us. If that's so then I got to say, they must be using fame the wrong way. Hell, give me some of that fame, I'll show them what to do with it.

Now I ain't lonely or lost. At least I don't think so. I got me a date. That's where I'm going right now. I'm waiting for the crosstown bus to get here so I can go pick her up. We going to the "Theatre." Can you believe that? Me, going to the theatre. But she said she likes theatre so I bought the tickets to make an impression. I like her and she likes me, I think. So who knows, things might work out. But you see while I'm standing here waiting all these women pass by and I get distracted. My mind start to work and I get to wondering how it might be. How it could be. How it ought to be. How it even will be. Oh man, my head just keep on spinning and spinning. And I keep dreaming and dreaming.

(*Pause*)

Know what the problem is? It ain't me. No, it ain't me at all. The problem is this city. There's too many people, too little space. Too much rushing around. Too much noise. Too many women . . . too little time. And definitely, not enough of *me*. Think about it and you'll see I'm right. Oh, oh, here comes my bus. Gotta go. Catch you all again, soon.

He leaves.

Whatever Happened to Warning Shots?

Lights change to suggest early evening. Traffic noises can be heard. When the lights come up, it's nighttime. Karen, a woman in her early forties in a police uniform (minus pistol), is sitting on a park bench. As she begins to speak, the sounds fade.

It's hard being a female cop out on these streets. In the precinct they call us "Officers" because by law they can't separate us by sexes. But once you hit the pavement all the rules change.

Give you an example: Few weeks ago I was walking my beat. Me and my partner. A group of young boys, late teens I would guess, passed by us. As they did one called out, "Hey, look, a bitch cop." Then another said: "Yhoo, Mama, what you planning to do with that thing on your hip. Shoot somebody? I got me a weapon, too," he continued. And I didn't have to look back to know he was grabbing his crotch. "Yeah. Only when this gun shoot bullets it bring life to the world. Not death."

What do you do about this kind of heckling? My partner wanted to go back and talk to the boys. I told him to "forget it." What would be the point? What are you going to do, teach them respect with the end of a billy club? Is it really their fault that they have no respect for women across the board? No matter what her position might be?

I got on the force because I thought I could change things. Yeah, laugh. Naive, right? Egotistical? Yeah, that too. Imagine one lone, individual woman thinking her presence in a situation could alter the outcome and even change things on a long-term basis. Now when I say it even I have to laugh.

As a girl, I grew up right here in Harlem. On these streets. In my neighborhood a three cop combo ruled the area like a reign of terror. We called them "the King Cole Trio." Two big white cops and a short little black one. If any mischief was going down and somebody called out "the King Cole Trio!" it suddenly got cool and people began to disperse. These guys kept law and order, but it was at a price. The price was fear, intimidation, and advantage taking. I can't say they ever took bribes because I know for a fact they didn't. But there are other ways of asserting your dominance.

I remember one day this guy, this drunk named Buster, was beating up his wife and somebody called the cops. When the Trio arrived Buster was dumb enough or drunk enough to give them an argument. After they took him aside and worked him over, they warned him not to go by his apartment till they said it was okay.

"Where am I supposed to sleep?" Buster asked. "In the gutters for all we care. Just don't come back here till we tell you, understand?" Buster shook his head.

After he left the little black cop went over to Buster's wife, Ruth, and said, "I'll be back 'round nine tonight, just to make sure he don't bother you." And before she could protest he said, "You called for police protection, now that's what you getting, Baby." And, of course, he was as good as his word. He arrived in his civvies a little after nine and proceeded to spend the night. Just for her "protection."

People around here have a low regard and distrust for the police and all we represent. And who can blame them? The good officer, the compassionate officer, the intelligent officer is so rare that his or her existence approaches being more of a rumor than a fact.

I joined up like I said to change things. To show that police officers could be fair and understanding as well as cruel and indifferent. Sometimes it works, sometimes it doesn't. But being a woman in most of these situations never helps. You walk into a fight, call out, "BREAK IT UP!", everybody ignores you. Or somebody calls out, "Why don't you go home and wash your husband's clothes, baby." And the altercation continues. But when you go in with your pistol out and pointed at somebody's eyeball suddenly they listen and things get very quiet. That's just the way it is, unfortunately.

(*Pause*)

I'm sitting here because I'm on a suspension-without-pay, pending an inquiry into my shooting of a seventeen-year-old boy. He was walking down the street smashing in the windshields of parked cars with a baseball bat. When I called for him to stop and drop the bat, he looked at me as though I was speaking a foreign language.

"Drop it!" I yelled at him again, this time going down on one knee with my pistol aimed straight at him.

"She won't shoot," somebody called from the crowd. "Hit her with the club! Yeah, bust her head open!" and this hulking lug came at me with his face contorted. I swear I aimed for his shoulder. But the bullet caught him square in the chest. On instinct, I pulled the trigger again. The second shot hit him in the stomach and he went flying back.

Seventeen, they told me later. That's how old he was. Seventeen. He looked to be more than that. And crazed. Well, it turns out that he was not only seventeen but retarded as well. The boy didn't have many brain cells working.

Now I'm being crucified in the press for killing a simple-minded boy whose only crime was destroying a bunch of inanimate objects.

I can't go home because there are civic groups demonstrating in front of my place calling me a murderer. While others are demanding my immediate dismissal from the force.

I joined up to do some good. And I can do a lot of good. Officers like myself are rare. And the force needs us. So I'm not going to quit. And I refuse to let them run me out of town. With these things you learn to play a waiting game. You lay low until it blows over or some new incident becomes the target of their outrage. Even my chief feels that way. He says the inquiry will just be a formality because obviously I behaved according to procedure. The other officers have taken up a collection to get me over the suspension period. So it's just a matter of time. Now all I have to do is wait.

Mavis comes rushing out. As she begins to talk the lights change. Sometime during the start of her monologue the policewoman rises slowly and exits.

Mavis #3

Mavis rushes in, and the lights change as she begins to talk.

You ever been in love so bad that that's all you think about
all day and all night? Well, that's the state I'm in and I got
to say I love it. Every morning I wake up, I wake up with a
smile. And every night I go to sleep feeling young again.

*Saxophone music begins and we see the man behind the scrim
again.*

I been seeing him more and more. Yes, yes, I'm talking
about Russell. Sometimes as often as three times a week. If
Ernie suspecting something he ain't saying nothing. I tell him
'bout all this family I visiting where I have to stay overnight
and he just say, "Alright, I'll see you when I see you."

My whole week I live for the nights when I can be
there. The loft is cold, the bed lumpy, the street outside is
noisy but—so what? And I don't mind his not talking. Just
being in the same room and with him is enough. I guess if
you asked what it is about him that getting me so excited,
I would have to say—I don't know. He don't do anything
different than other men do. But somehow when he do it
with me I feel warm and special.

I love him and that's a fact. He make me feel good
about myself. And about life. Better than I ever felt before,
that's for sure.

Oh Lord, I don't know why I'm in love. Maybe I need
to be in love. All I know is it feels good and I don't want it
to end. Ever.

*She exits just as an eccentrically dressed woman carrying a
sign enters.*

Marvin Gaye Died for Your Sins

Ruth, an eccentrically dressed woman in her forties, enters carrying a sign. The sign says Marvin Gaye Died for Your Sins. *She looks at Mavis going off then turns to the audience and begins to speak.*

Go on, go on all of you. That's right. That's it. Walk on by. Pretend that you don't hear it. Pretend that I ain't here.

MARVIN GAYE DIED FOR YOUR SINS! THAT'S WHAT I SAID: MARVIN GAYE DIED FOR YOUR SINS! Keep walking but I'm telling you the truth— Marvin Gaye died for your sins!

(*Pause*)

When I was a little girl growing up, the music you used to hear, songs you used to dance to was Ruby and the Romantics telling you "Our Day Will Come" or Diana Ross and the Supremes telling us "Ain't No Mountain High Enough." Boys had their heroes in James Brown— Godfather of Soul and Brook Benton, Crown Prince of Cool. But the one all of us could get together on, although nobody ever said it out loud, was Johnny Mathis who would sing "Chances Are" and "When Sunny Gets Blue" so soft and so sweet that when you standing there and dancing it's like there ain't nobody else in the whole wide world.

He was so much like a drug on our feelings and our minds that we didn't even call him by his real name. We used to call him "Johnny Mattress" because when you was finished listening to his song, that's all you was ready for— the mattress.

MARVIN GAYE DIED FOR YOUR SINS! THAT'S
WHAT HE DIED FOR, TO CLEANSE THE EVIL
FROM YOUR HEARTS. MARVIN GAYE DIED FOR
YOUR SINS!

(*Pause*)

New York is a city of twenty million people running in
all kinds of directions trying their best to catch up to life.
Some of them even leave that life on the streets long before
they even have a chance to catch their own breaths. Man I
know come up here in Harlem to live and work with his
own people he used to say. He was from the South and
went to divinity school. After he graduate they offered him
a position in the hometown church he was baptized in.
But he said, "No. Harlem is where I'm needed and where I
want to be." So he came here and worked with the kids
and people of this special neighborhood. And everybody
liked Reverend Al. Once in a while somebody would break
into his place and steal a camera or a TV. But once folks
put the word out who the stuff belonged to, it was always
brought back with a little note saying, "Sorry."

Reverend Al used to teach, give counsel, conduct ser-
vices, attend christenings, go to burials and also marry
people when they asked him. He used to say to me, "My
record isn't very good. Two out of every five couples I
marry either abandon each other or get divorced." But that
wasn't his fault. He always used to counsel the couple three
weeks before the ceremony on the responsibilities of the
Holy State of Matrimony. He couldn't be blamed if they
didn't want to listen. Kids nowadays act like they listening
but the truth of the matter is, they ain't hearing nothing at
all. But those statistics always used to make him sad.

Then one Sunday morning he told the congregation
that this was to be his last sermon. "I'm moving out of the
area and going down into midtown. I'm going to where
the responsibility of other peoples' lives won't bear so heav-
ily on me. I feel my work here has been in vain, so I'm

going where I can take some time to address some of my own needs."

He left and we gave him a grand send-off even though he was moving only a matter of a few miles.

The neighborhood got a new minister and we didn't hear nothing about Reverend Al for a couple of months. Then one day we heard he was dead. Some friends went looking for him over a weekend. When they found they couldn't reach him either by phone or by ringing his bell they asked the building super to use his passkey. He found Reverend Al on the floor with a knife stuck in his heart. The police say it was the work of a robber but they never caught the man.

We buried him here in Harlem in the yard next to the church. Now he will always be with us where we can love and protect his memory.

MARVIN GAYE DIED FOR YOUR SINS! YES HE DID! YES HE DID!

(*Pause*)

It's funny how we believe the same old lies and stories year after year even though we know what they telling us is so much bunk. And so much baloney. For example, they keep telling us that race relations between blacks and whites is improving, when I know for a fact that it getting worse. All you got to do is walk through the wrong neighborhood or wander into the wrong party and you'll find out how quick they is to let you know you don't belong. Mike Tyson is an ape which is why he was knocking everybody out so easily. Martin Luther King was a womanizer who supposedly cheated on his master's thesis so he shouldn't have a day named in his honor. Malcolm X was a junkie, fanatic, and pimp. So why should anybody take what he had to say seriously, or go to a movie made about his life. Of course we can see hundreds made about Billy the Kid and Jesse James. But Malcolm X—no.

The only black people who deserve respect is the ones white folks tell us we should admire. See, that's because we can't decide for ourselves or that's what they think. In our hearts and minds we still little children waiting to grow up. We haven't developed yet, so we can't make important decisions.

MARVIN GAYE DIED FOR YOUR SINS. . . . And that's a fact.

PLEASE COME BACK MARVIN GAYE: PLEASE COME BACK TO US NOW. WE NEED YOU MORE THAN EVER. WE NEED ALL OUR SAINTS AND SINNERS. WE CAN'T AFFORD TO LOSE ANY OF YOU. NOT A ONE. NOT MARTIN, NOT MEDGAR, NOT MALCOLM, AND ESPECIALLY NOT YOU MARVIN. WE LOVE YOU AND WE NEED YOU. PLEASE COME BACK TO US NOW. AND SING YOUR SONGS OF LOVE AND HEALING.

MARVIN GAYE DIED FOR YOUR SINS! You hearing me? MARVIN GAYE DIED FOR YOUR SINS! REPENT! REPENT, BEFORE IT'S TOO LATE! MARVIN GAYE DIED FOR YOUR SINS! MARVIN GAYE DIED FOR YOUR SINS! TELL ME I'M CRAZY, TELL ME I'M GONE! BUT I KNOW WHEREOF I SPEAK. MARVIN GAYE DIED FOR YOUR SINS! MARVIN GAYE DIED FOR YOUR SINS!

She continues this as the lights begin to fade and she exits. As soon as the stage goes black Marvin Gaye's recording "Mercy, Mercy, Mercy Me" is heard.

ACT TWO

The Collector

Bosco, a man in his late twenties who is dressed shabbily, comes out carrying a huge plastic bag that contains hundreds of beer and soda cans. He walks across the stage carrying his cumbersome burden. Somewhere on the way he trips, the bag tips, and several cans roll out. Quickly, he scrambles to retrieve them.

Ooops . . . (*He calls urgently to somebody offstage*) Hey! Hey! Don't step on that can!" (*It's too late*) It's okay, what's one nickel more or less, right? . . . Well, the same to you, man! In spades! . . . (*Now to the immediate audience*) "The poor are always with you," right? . . . "If they can't find bread, let them eat peach cobbler" . . . "Don't tell me these people can't find jobs. Especially the young ones, when everyday I see want ads in the papers. Pages and pages of them." . . . "Something's happening in our society. These young people don't want to work. They want to indulge themselves, swell our welfare rolls, and when they're processed out, walk our streets indigent, creating an unsightly form of human debris. Something must be done about this ever-growing army before they completely take over the streets and begin entering our homes."
(*Pause*)
Is that what you really think? That I want to enter your homes? . . . (*He laughs*) There used to be a time when the phrase was, "It's alright to talk to a colored. But would you want your daughter marrying one?" Things have changed in these here United States of Freedom and Democracy. Now the phrase is: "It's alright to feed the

homeless but how'd you like to have one sleeping in your bed?" . . . (*He pauses and shakes his head*)

Let me tell you something. Nobody homeless started out to be homeless. A man without pride didn't start out that way. Look at me, when I came to this city I had big things on my mind. Dreams of career and success just like any other man. And I came from good stock. My peoples is out of Ohio, and they even got property there. When I told them I was going to New York, everybody was against it. They said the city was cold, the people hard, and the life not fit for a rat to survive in. But I didn't have no choice. Wasn't nothing for me in that tiny town but the same ole, same ole. So I got on the Greyhound and I jumped out on Times Square. Times Square, nerve center of the great Metropolis! (*Sings*) "Come and meet those dancing feet. On the Avenue I'm taking you to: 42nd Street" . . . Damn, them lights had me dazzled right from that first night. I couldn't get enough of them so I just walked around the area night after night after night just staring at this world wondering how I could be a part of it. Didn't have nobody to guide me so I had to talk to strangers. Now strangers are a funny breed. If they can't use you or abuse you, they'll misguide you. And that's what I think happened to me. A bunch of strangers led me and misled me until I didn't know which way was up.

Had me a few jobs but none of them ever work out. Lived in a few places too but had to leave when I couldn't pay rent. Didn't want to leave, but had to leave. You know how that can be.

Went with a bunch a women. Two even wanted me to marry them. But I said no. Hell, how am I going to take care of somebody when I can't even take care of myself? Besides which, those chicks wasn't what I figured I would wind up with when I came to this city. I had dreams of achieving bigger things, making better connections. I go home married to women like that, people would laugh after all the boasting I done. Nooo—a man got to hold onto his dreams if he ever want to amount to anything in this world. I may not have much, but I sure got my dreams. Yes sir, yes sir, I got them in spades.

(*Pause*)

You see me here collecting cans and you figure "He's a lost cause. Another loser who wouldn't make it in this city." Well, you figuring wrong. I ain't dead and I got a lot of future in front of me. This condition I'm in is just a temporary state. Just a small setback for a man on his way to a lot of big places. I been in this city now going on eight years and I got it all doped out. I know how to beat it and make it kiss my foot. All I need now is to regroup, get a nest egg together, and start over again. And these cans I'm collecting is what gon' turn the trick for me. I been walking all over the city collecting them every place I can. Then I store them in a secret hiding place. No, I don't turn them in. If I did I'd just spend the money on food and liquor. No, I just store them. It's like having money in the bank. One day I'm going to have a million cans. I already have over five thousand. That's when I'll turn them in. . . . One million cans at a nickel a piece. Figure it out for yourself.

What am I going to do with the money once I turn the cans in? I could tell you cause I got it all figured out. I ain't like those people who win the million dollar lottery and suddenly don't know what the hell to do with their lives. No sir. I got it all mapped out to the smallest detail. But I don't think I'm going to tell you. Want to know why? If I did then you'll be as smart as me, won't you? No, a man got to keep his dreams. But he got to keep his secrets too.

So you are right. "The poor is always with us" . . . Thank God I ain't one of them.

(*He picks up his bag and sings as he exits*)

"Happy Days are here again. The sky above is clear again" . . .

Lifetime on the Streets

A man over fifty comes out looking at a ring on his third finger and playing with it. He walks with a slight limp.

See this ring? Tell you how I got it. A goddamn derelict walk up to me in front of Willoby's Men Store. I wasn't doing anything, just standing there looking at the stuff they got in the window. But I musta look like a mark. Anyway, this fool come over to me and ask if I want to buy a real diamond ring for twenty bucks. I look this man up and down. I must look to him like some kinda tourist. Me, buy a diamond ring from a person that look and smell like that?

"You talking to me?" I ask this man.

(*Then imitating the Derelict*)

"Yes. I'm offering you a genuine 14-karat diamond ring for twenty dollars. Used to belong to an old aunt a mine. Carried it around for years as a keepsake because the old lady bring me up and I always felt grateful to her. Now things've gone bad and I got to sell it if I want to keep body and soul together."

Touching story, right? Only it's a lie. And you a fool if you believe it. That smelly bastard probably knock some old lady down and pull it off her finger. Or maybe even break her finger to get it. I looked at this fool and was going to tell him, "Get the hell away from me." Then another thought come to my mind. "Teach him something about survival on these streets."

So I put my hand in my pocket like I was going to reach for money, then I say, "How do I know this ring is diamond? How do I know you ain't lying to me?"

"Show you something," he said, holding up the ring.
"You know only a diamond can cut glass. Right? Well,
look at this." Then he made a deep scratch mark in the
glass a Willoby's window.
   "Let me see that ring," I said to him.
   "Here." The fool gave it to me. I hold it up to the light
and look at it. Then I put it on my finger and look at it
some more.
   "Fit good, right."
   "Fit damn good."
   "Twenty dollars."
   I look at the fool. "You got to be joking," I said to
him. "Twenty dollars! You expect me to pay you twenty
dollars for a ring that already belong to me?"
   "What you talking about?"
   "This ring. This same ring. This is now mine. An old
family heirloom that used to belong to the old woman that
brought me up. Aunt Della . . . Now if I was you I'd get
away from here before I call that cop down the street and
tell him you trying to steal my ring." Man look at me like he
couldn't believe I was saying that to him. "Dirty and funky
as you is I wouldn't be surprised if he don't call some kind of
exterminator company to fumigate you before putting you
in jail. So you better go now. And I'll tell you something
else. This hand in my pocket touching something that'll
bring you a lot more misery than losing a diamond ring."
Of course, I was only holding my comb, but that fool didn't
know that. . . . He look to see if I was bluffing. When I
stepped closer to him, he realized that I wasn't, so he just
said, "Man you don't live right. God gon' punish you one a
these good days. You a Brother ain't got no feelings for
another Brother down on his luck. God gon' punish you for
sure." And with that went on shuffling down the street.
   (*Pause*)
   See, people want to live out here on the streets but
they don't know the rules. The rules is a *Eye for a eye* and

Survival of the fittest. Which is to say: *The smartest.* Take smarts to live out here, else you'll be dead in a week.

(*Pause*)

These streets is my home. Ain't never had no other. 'Course I don't mean I sleep here. I don't look like no damn bum, do I? Hell, no. I got me a fine li'l apartment up there on St. Nicholas Avenue. Been in there now damn near thirty years. Landlords come and go but I stay on forever.

Lots a women pass through that place, but none ever stayed on. None ever been invited. What I want to be married for? I'm having enough of a good time being just as I am.

When I hit this place I was a green lad, like all them others you see around looking for two things. Good times and an easy way to make some money. Found out early too much liquor and dope only make you a fool. And crime? Real crime don't pay. To make it pay you got to be organized. And even when you organized you always looking over your shoulder at the people around you. So, the only thing to live by is your wits. If you got them.

Used to fool around with a girl named Gloria, had herself a nice job and money in the bank. Only she didn't believe in no bank. So she used to keep the money hidden in places around the apartment. She wasn't very pretty but I mess with her from time to time because she'd let me get my fingers on some a that money. But you see I was a boy and didn't know how to secure my business. So after I got ahold of her money I wouldn't come around again for months. The woman of course got wise to that and start refusing to give me any money. Now she wasn't no fool, and what I had to offer she wanted to get. Even if it was only once in a while. So she didn't up and refuse to give me money. She just say to me that she didn't have any.

Now this is where the wit came in. I didn't say nothing either and we'd get to doing our business on that bed.

Then I'd wait till it was going hot and heavy. When she was practically in a trance. Then I'd say, soft and loving like: "Where's the money? Tell me darling, tell me where it is." And outta that ecstasy and excitement, she would say, "In my galoshes. In my galoshes." Then when she fell asleep I'd take the money and leave. Simple as that.

(*Brief pause as though the story is over*)

Problem was, one night she woke up just as I was leaving. She screamed and chased me down the avenue with a bread knife. Three o'clock in the morning. Wasn't many people on the street. But there was enough to laugh and make noise at this spectacle. I turn a corner and she musta been close to me cause I heard a swish and felt a burn on my butt. Damn woman had slash and cut a piece off my behind. I could feel the blood running down my leg. So I wave for a cab and ask him to take me to the hospital. When I got there they fixed me up like new. In less than a week I was back on the street with money in my pockets. Maybe my butt hurt a little bit, but my pockets was smiling like a clown.

Did a bit of hustling at one time. Made some money at it too. Bought me a big car and hired a man to drive it. Late one night he was taking me home when this other player's car speed right by us. I said to my driver, "If you don't catch that car and pass it in the next five minutes, you don't got no job driving for me and that's a fact." The man said, "Yes sir" and put his foot on the gas. The next thing I know the car wind up smack into the pole of an elevated train station. He went through the windshield. And me, they had to cut away parts of the car door to get me out. My hip and my leg got busted. That's why today I got one leg a little shorter than the other.

Some years later I was in a card game. I had a fine hand for cards. My daddy showed me how. Man never showed me much but he did show me that. I was winning when one of the boys accused me of cheating. So I said,

"That's it. I'm quitting." And I put out my hand to pick up my money. Well, that boy stamp a knife down. Took off my little finger. But I did get a hold of the money and out before the pain got so bad I had to go to the doctor. Speed and agility. That's another thing you need out on these streets.

I actually had a job once. I don't like working though. Never did. This job was with a veterinarian. A white fellow who used to take care of this dog Boo I had. I told him how I found Boo on the streets eating scraps, ribs all sticking out and everything. He told me I did a good job with Boo and maybe I had a feel for working with animals. Said he needed somebody to take care of the animals while he went on vacation. Wasn't nothing serious. Just feed the animals, pet them. And look to see they was doing fine. When he came back he said I did a wonderful job. Offered to take me on full-time. Teach me to recognize when they're sick and what medicine to give them.

I thought about it for a minute, then I told him no. I like animals and all, but the money wasn't enough.

(*Pause*)

I been on these streets all of my life. Ain't never regret it. Sure it take its toll sometimes. Couple years ago a guy broke a whisky bottle over my head just after I got a haircut. So I had nothing up here to cushion the blow. Twenty-six stitches is what it took to close up the wound. I still can feel the scar when I comb my hair. But other than that I'm in good health and I got a lot of amusing memories.

This ring look like it might really be diamond. I might get me a hundred dollars for it at the pawnshop. Maybe . . . even more. So don't tell me I don't know how to make it on these streets. This place been good to me in all kinds of ways.

He exits as Mavis comes out. Lights change.

Mavis #4

Well, I went and done it. Took me a while and a whole lot of thinking. But when that was over I just up and did it. I told Ernie about Russ and about how I been feeling. After I finished telling him, he got up from his chair and walked over to the window and ask: "So what you want to do?"

"Get a divorce," I told him.

"Why?"

"Because I love Russ."

"Oh, I see."

"Yes," I told him. "I love him and I want to live with him. So I'm moving out."

"Oh, I see," he said. "I guess your mind is made up." Then he didn't say anything for a long while. Just stood by that window staring out on the street.

When I told Russ about it, he ask me why. "Because it the right thing," I said. "And because I love you."

"You sure about that?" he asked.

"I'm more sure about that than I am about anything, Russ. I think I love you more than I love myself." He didn't say anything. He just stood there looking at me.

(*Pause*)

I been posing for him these last few weeks of going up there. He already paint one nude study of me. And is working on another. It was during them sessions that I got to thinking how nice it would feel to be here all the time. Russ could paint and I could work. And everything could be just fine. Just him and me, me and him. (*Closes her eyes*) Hmmm . . .

(*Pause*)
I'm still home with Ernie, but it won't be for long now. Two, three more days at the most. . . . I can't wait.

Saxophone music is heard as the lights fade and Mavis exits.

Streetwalker

A spotlight finds a man in his mid thirties dressed in a suit sitting on a bench. He puts his hand up to shield himself from the blinding light. When he does the glare (in his eyes) softens as the whole stage illuminates. As it does he rises and moves toward the audience.

I did something today I guess I shouldn't've done. I went to a porno theatre. . . . Now with a wife and two girlfriends on the side, you'd think I'd have enough pornography in my life. Why would I want to see it up on a screen? Maybe I was bored. And also there was another reason. . . . Anyway this wasn't your standard porn. This was a gay theatre I wandered into—on purpose, if you follow my meaning. The sign said *With an All-Male Cast* and I plunked down my six dollars. I'll tell you why. A few days ago I went to the funeral of a friend who was gay. He had been killed by somebody he brought home with him. Some trash he picked up off the streets or out of some bar. I knew he did things like that and when I asked him about the possible dangers he said he had no fear. "Life is a risk that we all take when we wake up in the morning. If we start worrying about danger we would never leave the house."

I guess we've all seen from time to time stories in the papers about homosexual murders. But I never thought it could happen to any friend of mine. And never thought the facts about somebody's death could be so ugly. But I won't go into that now. It's enough to say that at the funeral I was distressed. Even disoriented.

At least that's the excuse I give myself. Or perhaps as many gay men like to say: "There are damn few who aren't curious."

Was I curious? Am I curious? To tell the truth, I don't know. I guess like every other middle-class, middle-aged, middle-educated, middle-messed-up fool in this city, I live in the secret fear that one morning I'll wake up and find that I'm a screaming queen. And that I've been one all my life but just didn't know it.

(*Pause*)

Anyway, I went into this porno house and everything was strange. I walked into the theatre and there were a bunch of guys standing back looking at the film and making it with each other. I don't know why I'm saying this, but I got the distinct feeling that they'd all been strangers ten minutes before.

I sat down and began to look at the picture. The theatre must've had forty or fifty people in it, all men, but very few were sitting. Most were walking up and down the aisle, smoking, stopping every now and then to check out somebody in one of the seats. One or two stopped by me but I focused my attention to the action on the screen, as a means of discouraging them.

The story, what I could make of it, was simplicity itself. Just the barest suggestion of a plot for them to include the most sexually explicit scenes one can imagine. There was virtually no dialogue. Just a lot of sound effects and loud pounding music. Music that seemed to go right through your brain. I think it was music that was making the strongest impression on me. I kept watching the action and thinking, "Damn, don't these people ever get tired or bored?" The action was so mechanical, so sexless, and so joyless. Or so it seemed to me, anyway.

Now while I was thinking all this a heavyset guy sat next to me and kept saying in a soft low voice, "Hey . . . Hey, look. I got something to show you." When I finally glanced over he was sitting there exposed, handling himself. So I got up, moved and sat in another empty area. I wasn't there five minutes when this skinny little guy sat next to me and began smoking like a chimney. A whole empty theatre and this bastard has to sit next to me. Smoking. I wanted to say, "Hey faggot, get the hell away from me." But I also wanted to go someplace with him. A dark alley, or a motel room somewhere. And after we got there and he started smiling and touching and taking his clothes off, I would start beating him. With my fists, my feet or anything I could find. A stick, a club, a section of pipe. Anything I could find. I would beat him till I was tired and he was no more. I would beat him till the anger, frustration, insanity, or whatever it is I was feeling left my body.

And for some reason, I thought it would make me feel better.

It was a funny series of feeling I had, trying to figure what to do about this man. This queer. This homo. This piece of—well, it's enough to say I was confused. So I did the most sensible thing. I got up and walked out of the theatre.

When I hit the sidewalk I was still in a rage. I didn't know why. I've never hated homosexuals or felt they shouldn't be allowed to live in the world. Hell, I'm black and there are those who say I shouldn't be allowed to exist because of my color. So who am I to make a judgment? And I've never thought that way. Yet there I was walking around mad and wanting to hurt somebody.

(*Pause*)

I'll tell you the truth. I think it had something to do with honesty. I went in there to be an observer. An outsider, but the situation demanded that I participate. Or leave. Honestly, what could I have said to any of those men who propositioned me? "Leave me alone, faggot"? Their natural answer would've had to be, "If you didn't want to be approached, why are you in here?" See what I'm saying? It gets very confused when you start seeing all sides of things.

Anyway I've been walking around for a couple hours now trying to figure out all these feelings. Especially the overwhelming urge to pound my fist into something. I think it had to do with the movie, the loud music they played in the background. And all those graphic scenes of aggression and dominance. There was something very Nazi-*Night-of-the-Long-Knives* about it. And the way it had worked on me. I left that theatre not wanting to have sex with a man, but maybe wanting to kill one.

Is that what my friend Allan ran into when he brought a stranger into his home? Is that why there are so many stories of violence and death in homosexual connections? I don't know. I don't have any answers. I'm just lost. So I guess I'll keep walking the streets until I come up with a few. Because I know I can't go home right now. Not when I'm feeling like this. (*He holds up both hands, which are shaking violently*)

Suicide Note

Jenna, a black model in her early thirties, comes forward wearing some fashionable outfit. She's carrying a bottle of wine and a glass. She sits, pours herself some wine, and takes a sip.

I don't mind admitting that I like wine. I like it and I drink it a lot. It makes me feel good. And that's what everybody wants in life isn't it? To feel good.

People tell me I'm lucky. All I have to do is stand back and let photographers take pictures of me in somebody's latest design and I get paid money for it. Sometimes even a lot. . . . Other girls have to scrub floors, teach school, mind other people's babies, or answer telephones. But me, all I have to do is stand here, turn there, walk like a pony up and down some ramp while those flashbulbs keep going and a lot of people in glasses point at you.

How'd the instructor in modeling school put it? "Proud, darling. Let them sense how proud you are." So I stand there looking proud and aloof. But I hate it.

My father was a mailman who had a smile for every door he delivered a letter to. Everybody used to say, "What a nice man Mr. Wilkin is." But at night when he came home he would drink a bottle of rye and yell at Mom and us kids.

"I got to be nice all day on the outside. Don't expect me to be that way all night in my house, too."

If we let him drink he wouldn't scream at us or beat us so much. So we let him, although we could see what it was doing to him.

After he died, my mother started to drink without telling anybody. She would mix vodka with a half glass of water and sip at it all day, while she was doing whatever it was she was doing.

At the same time she took up religion and would have the radio playing hymn music all day and into the night. Then the TV would start going with some Reverend somebody or other telling us "Your only salvation is in the word of the Lord" over and over again.

In the background as she remembers, we hear faint sounds of religious music and then some TV preacher talking.

My sister Jaunice said, "I'm getting outta this crazy house" and married this forty-year-old guy although she was only nineteen. Raymond, my brother, got into trouble with the law and had to join the army so as to escape going to jail.

The woman at the agency said, "I like your pictures. Come to New York. I think we can do something for you." So I packed my bags and went.

In New York I got married because I couldn't stand being a single woman in this profession. Everyone assumes that because you pose in evening gowns or lingerie they should put their hands on you.* And it wasn't just the men. There are a lot of women, too, who will promise you everything. Then give you liquor and dope in hopes of getting their hands all over you.

(*Stops and drinks some wine*)

If it wasn't for this wine I don't know what I would do. People say it will start affecting my looks. SO BIG DEAL! For some reason they really think I would care.

(*Pause*)

When I married Joey, I thought things would be different. He said they would be. He was managing a rock

---

*If slides are being used in this production, we should see some shots of the model in evening gowns, sexy lingerie, and so forth, here.

band and making a lot of money. But he was away a lot of times, too. With the band.

He would come back off the road and all he'd want to do is party. I wanted a baby, but all he kept saying was: "Later, honey. There'll be lots of time for babies later."

Then one night at a party in a penthouse he went out on the terrace and looked down on the lights of the city for a long time. Then without saying anything he climbed up on the ledge and jumped. Thirty-four stories before he hit the pavement.

I wasn't there. People told me about it. Said he was high, that's why it happened.

Guys who we were close to offered support. Two even offered to marry me. One guy, a singer, even offered me a 50-50 split from his latest record if I would just move in with him. But I wasn't hurting for money. Joey left a lot, till one day the cops came in and took it all. Including the furniture. They said Joey had been selling drugs to his musicians and to a lot of other people, too. I didn't know anything about that. But everybody said it was true. People sometimes have secrets they never tell you about. So, to make a living I had to go back to work. Modeling.

Long pause. Cocktail lounge music is heard. She drinks some more wine.

His name is Brendan and he's the one pleasant memory I have in all this misery. He was sad from the first day I met him. It was in a bar. He liked the same kind of wine I did. We went back to his apartment and because he couldn't do anything else we drank and talked.

"Liquor's made me impotent," he said. "For the longest while I thought it was a blessing. But when I look at you I realize it's a curse."

We used to often lie in the same bed, talk and drink till we fall asleep. I love that man although our love can only take us but so far. Sex isn't part of our relationship. But then again, I've always thought sex overrated anyway.

(*Pause*)

They had to lock Mama away. For her own protection they said. Ray is still in the Army and Jaunice's got four children with three different men. Our family is so split up we can't even get together at Christmastime.

I haven't been intimate with a man in close to five years. Every day I wake up I wonder why nothing ever excites me. The whole thing seems like just a big waste of time.

They took Brendan to the hospital. The doctors say he won't be coming out.

This has been a bad ride and it won't ever stop unless I stop it. So that's what the answer is. Put an end to something that probably shouldn't've started in the first place. Brendan is unconscious with tubes sticking out of him. He won't know. And the rest of the people I know won't even care.

So, I'll just finish this bottle of wine. And then it'll be time.

She takes another sip as the light fades.

The Bag Lady

A woman in rags enters the stage pushing a shopping cart full of old clothes, newspapers, and other debris. A well-dressed man in his thirties carrying a briefcase enters from the opposite side. As the old lady seems headed straight for him, he steps out of the way to let her by. As she passes she glances at him quickly and mutters something angrily under her breath and goes on by.
Man, to the audience, after the old lady exits.

A curious thing just happened here and perhaps you noticed it. That woman that just almost hit me and then went muttering by? She and I are related. That Bag Lady? You don't believe me do you? But it's true. That woman, that bag lady is my mother. I guess I should have some emotion about it. And I do. But it's buried so deep inside that now when I talk about it my tone comes out as indifferent. I assure you that I'm anything but.

Now before I tell you about my mother I guess I should tell you something about myself. The name's Richardson. Burton Richardson. I'm the vice president in charge of advertising for a large breakfast cereal company. My salary—Well, never mind what my salary is. It's substantial, as you can well imagine. My wife and I have a house in New Rochelle and an apartment here in the city. We have no children but we're thinking of adopting. Our circle of friends include a state senator, a couple of judges, two well-known painters and a police commissioner. I'm telling you this not to appear snobbish but to give you an accurate picture of who I am. And how I'm situated.

As a kid growing up in Florida we didn't have much.

But we weren't impoverished either. My brother and I grew up with a proper respect for money and the things it could do for us. And for education as a means of getting to that money. Our father was a blue-collar worker who always stressed the power of mind over body. He worked for the city as a laborer. Whenever he came home his clothes were always sweaty and his hands crusted with dirt. "You see," he would say to my brother and me, "if you learn your lessons you won't have to do this for a living. You can be one of those people sitting behind a big desk talking on the telephone all day. Then driving a big car home at night. Me, I didn't have those opportunities. My people were farmers just come to town. So I had to take what work I could get."

My father might've been uneducated, but he wasn't without ambition. He, and my mother too—they worked hard and made sure my brother and I both had a college education. When we left home, I went into the army, then came here to live. So did my brother, Rodney.

(*Pause*)

I had just returned home from work one evening when the phone rang. It was their next-door neighbor telling me my father had died. My brother and I rushed back and found our mother strangely composed but distant. She told us how Daddy had died as though it was something that had happened to a distant relative.

After the funeral she still was behaving this way, so we thought it might be a good idea to bring her to New York. She said she had always wanted to go to New York. It was a trip she and Pop had been in the process of planning.

Rodney was married, so she couldn't live with him. I was single at the time with a big apartment. So it wasn't a problem. She would live with me.

The first six months we did a lot of things together. But mostly we talked. Actually she talked. Always about Pop and how funny he could be when no one else was around.

I had to work during the day so she was home alone a lot. When I asked what she did, she'd say, "walked." One afternoon just by sheer accident I met her at the edge of Central Park sitting on a bench. She was talking to two men who didn't look very clean.

That evening when I asked her who they were she shrugged and said, "Friends."

I called Rodney and told him what I was beginning to perceive. For this wasn't the only clue I had. She had taken to getting up early in the morning and leaving the apartment around six. One day I followed her. She met with a group of derelicts and seemed quite comfortable in their company. More comfortable, in a funny way, than she had ever seemed with Rodney or myself. I also noticed she was dressing less and less decently. Not dirty exactly. But also not clean.

Rodney refused to believe the transformation I told him was beginning to take place.

"Not Mama. Not our mother," he kept saying. "She's got too much sense of herself. She's got too much pride."

"Then how do you explain what it is I've been telling you?"

He paused for a minute: "If this is really happening, we have to put her away," he said. We can't have her running around the street acting like a crazy woman." . . . I didn't agree. We nearly came to blows over it. He insisted that at least she see a doctor and I finally agreed.

After he left I told my mother what we talked about. She sat on the bed just looking at me like she couldn't understand a word of what I was saying. Finally, I said, "How do you feel about it?" She said, "I'm not happy here," in that same distant manner she used to describe Poppa's heart attack.

"What do you want to do?" I asked her.

"Go," she said. "Go away from here," she said.

"Where?"

"To find Bob." Bob was my father.

"How will you manage?"

"I'll manage," she said. "Don't worry about me."

"What about money and stuff?"

"I don't need any—I'll be fine." She touched my hand and went into the bedroom to sleep.

(*Pause*)

We didn't plan a time for her to leave but somehow I knew she'd be gone when I woke up.

Rodney wanted to send the police after her. I refused to let him do that. We experienced a period of coolness between us, and then that passed. Now we're back to being brothers.

That woman I passed isn't my mother. But then again, one can never be sure. A lot of years have passed. For all I know, my mother's probably dead. But then again maybe not. There are so many of those women out there. I tend to think of all of them as Mama. Figuring that one of these days, one of them just might be.

Lights fade.

Mavis #5

Excuse me . . . excuse me. I's looking for a store. A beauty shop that used to be around the corner on Courtland Avenue. A woman there, Miss Bertha, knowed how to do a person's hair just right. Now that woman and the place is gone. And my hair is just a mess. Look at it, all sticking out and crazy. Miss Bertha knowed what to do.

I'm sitting here because to tell you the truth, I don't know what to do. Night coming fast and I got no place to go except the empty loft of a man I used to know. Man was a painter. His name was Russell Baxter. This man didn't like to talk much but he had a lot of paintings. All around. Paintings of naked women.

(*Stops*)

But I don't want to talk about that. That's an old-time story everybody knows. What I want to talk about is a woman who got married too young to a man who had his own habits and knowed how to hide his feelings. This man—

(*Stops*)

No!—I don't want to talk about that either. Ain't nothing to talk about. Just as much as there ain't nothing to go back to.

(*Passionately, to the audience*)

How is it our men can't admit to their feelings? Why is it all of them got to act like they need to be strong. And why is it that being strong mean you got to be cold. And without any emotion. Does anybody know the answer? . . . I say to a man, "I love you," and he look at me and say,

"You sure?" . . . I tell another one I'm leaving after years and years of marriage and all he can say is, "That's a shame." There got to be more feeling. Got to be more heart. I know it because I feel it. Feel it till it choking me and I can hardly breathe.

That Sunday afternoon when I came like a fool carrying my suitcases, my heart was pumping, and my breath was short. I was changing my life. Turning over a new page and I was so excited. I push open the door and right away I knew something was wrong. The whole place was empty except for the mattress in the corner and the old kitchen table with two creaky chairs. But the curtains, the boxes, the paintings, and the books—all gone. I look around for clothes, they was gone too. How could this happen? What was going on? . . . I was here yesterday. We talked. I told him how good it would be, just him and me together. I asked him about them other women in the paintings, and told him I would be the last one he'd ever have to paint since I was going to be with him forever.

We drank wine and talked about the afternoon when I was walking around looking for Miss Bertha's. That was only three months ago. I was telling him how I never used to like Harlem and now how I come to love every foot of the place, in spite of the fact that there's too many old buildings. And too many poor people walking the streets.

(*Pause*)

Could I have scared him? Is that what it was? . . . Man didn't leave a note or anything. Just the keys to the front door on the kitchen table. . . . The fat man who live down the way look at me strange when I knocked on his door. He was a friend of Russell so it was only natural for me to ask if he knowed anything about him. . . . He didn't. All he could say is that Russell is like a bird in flight. "When he came, he came out of nowhere. Now he's gone—who knows?" . . . He invited me for a cup of coffee and we sat for an hour just talking. After I told him about my husband and why I couldn't go back home he said, "Harlem ain't a bad place. You just have to get used to it."

(*Long pause*)

I been sleeping in the loft and fixing it up. See, I don't believe Russell gone for good. It don't stand up to reason that a man would just pick up and leave a place he call home on less than a day's notice. He musta had some reason to go. Something musta called him so fast he didn't even have time to leave a note. But he gon' be back. I know that. It's just a matter of time.

In the meantime, I plan to keep looking for that beauty shop. Because I want to look good when he come back. And Miss Bertha is a woman who knows how to make a person look good.

But do me a favor. If you see Russell, tell him I didn't go nowhere. Tell him I'm right here where he left me. Waiting. And—er—tell him to hurry back. Okay? Thanks. Thanks a lot.

She sits.

Interlude

We hear a crack of thunder. Lights flash then settle to a bleak hard white. At this point several characters that we've seen before come out and begin to wander about the stage. They enter one by one, and speak some fragment of a previous monologue (3 or 4 sentences) and then wind up frozen in a position.

Once again the sound of thunder is heard.

Note: It is up to the director to choose the characters he wants to recall. Obviously, everyone can't return so a selection must be made. And from those characters the monologue segments should be selected.

New Ice Age #2

The Derelict reenters and looks at the frozen figures. Moves around investigating them a bit.

Damn. Didn't take long, did it? Freeze done set in, and it looks like the only living person or thing here is me. But I don't like being alone. It's lonely. . . . Damn, now I can go anyplace I want. Any restaurant or store. Places where they used to get excited and push me out the door the minute I walk in.

(*Moving forward, moving directly to the audience*)

Why you all like that? And now see what done happen. You all is gone, and who's left behind? Me. Poor old no-account me. "The meek shall inherit the earth," the Bible say. And for the longest while it didn't look like it would turn out to be true.

(*Getting even closer to the audience*)

Now, tell me the truth. When you all was building all these empires outta concrete, glass, and steel you didn't think I would be the one to wind up with all of it, did you? Figure it was for your children. Figure it was for future generations, right? Only thing is you killed all the future. Poisoned all the future generations. Couldn't kill me. Couldn't poison me 'cause you never thought about me. Never even noticed me. Only yourselves and what you thought you was achieving . . . Damn. But I got to say that I'm lost. . . . Didn't nobody ever ask me, as a member of the Meek, if I wanted to inherit the earth. Well, I'll tell you. I didn't and I don't. This place is filthy, dirty, polluted, covered over with plastic, cement, and garbage. Who want to own something like that? Who want to live in a place like this? Look around. Ask yourselves the same questions. Am I wrong?

But I'm stuck, ain't I? . . . City full a frozen people standing around like statues. Not one able to move his mouth to say, "Good morning." Or give you the time of day. Go into the stores, turn on the TVs, and it's rerun after rerun. Same things over and over. Same people smiling at you. Same pretty girls in bikinis jumping up and down telling you to buy something. Same people on the game shows winning the same useless money. Same news reports over and over and over again.

Maybe that's what hell is . . . or maybe it ain't the world that change. Maybe it's me. Maybe I made the trip from one world to the next and didn't even know it. Damn, I didn't even think of that. Here I am telling you 'bout the world that you done create when maybe it's a world only personal to me. A world created outta my sins and bad deeds where I alone have to wander about forever and ever. . . . Never even thought of it. What happened? Did I freeze to death while sitting on that park bench? Or did I get hit by a car? Fall down a manhole maybe? I don't remember anything.

(*Looks around at the figures*)

But it's real, ain't it? I'm in a real place with real people. Only they won't move. They won't change. They won't even rot. They gon' just stay like this forever and ever. And I'm stuck here with them talking to myself. Can you think of a worse punishment for anybody?

(*Pause*)

I have an idea. Maybe if I stay here long enough I'll get to be one a these frozen statues, too. Because clearly there ain't nothing to live for. Ain't nothing to hope for either.

He sits for the longest while. Then from behind the scrim the sax player begins to blow.

Damn. Is my ears playing tricks on me? Am I hearing what I think I'm hearing? Is there really somebody else left alive here?
(*Rising*)
Yes. Yes!
(*He looks around*)
I can't see who it is but I know they're out there somewhere. Some place close, too.
(*Suddenly excited*)
Just a matter of time before I find that other person. Just a matter of time. See, see, you didn't believe me but— I told you there was hope.

He moves in the direction of the sound, and suddenly freezes midstride. The saxophone blows wildly. Lights fade.

programs distributed in connection with performances of the play, and in all instances in which the title of the play appears for purposes of advertising, publicizing, or otherwise exploiting the play.

The name of the author must appear on a separate line, in which no other name appears, immediately beneath the title.